TEXAS
Hometown Cookbook

Bluebonnets abound in Spring

Pumpjacks are a familiar site on the Texas landscape

TEXAS
Hometown Cookbook

by **Sheila Simmons** and **Kent Whitaker**

Great American Publishers
www.GreatAmericanPublishers.com
TOLL-FREE 1.888.854.5954

Great American Publishers

171 Lone Pine Church Road • Lena, MS 39094

TOLL-FREE **1-888-854-5954 • www.GreatAmericanPublishers.com**

ISBN 978-1-934817-04-9

Printed in the United States of America

15 14 13 12 11 10 9

by **Sheila Simmons & Kent Whitaker**

Designed by Roger & Sheila Simmons

Front cover photos: Food (Rusty's Salt 'n Pepper Steaks with Bean Salsa) © Newedel; Bull Rider © Rick Hyman/iStockphoto.com; Big Bend National Park © Yenwen Lu istockphoto.com • Back cover photos: Food (Baked Strawberry Flan) © Tobik shutterstock.com; Freckles (Poteet Strawberry Festival Mascot) © Poteet Strawberry Festival • Page 2: Bluebonnets ©Design Pics/thinkstock; Pumpjacks ©Ginae McDonald/iStock-photo/thinkstock • Page 6: Dog costumes, Texas Blueberry Festival; Strawberry mascot, Poteet Strawberry Festival; Dutch oven, Harry Thomas/istockphoto/thinkstock; Ribs, Texas Reds Steak & Grape Festival; Tomaotes, Tomato Festival; Ferris wheel, Fulton Oysterfest. Boy fishing, Fish Day

Chapter opening photos: Appetizers p9 © David Smoth/iStockphoto/thinkstock • Breads p21 © Jaimie Duplass/iStockphoto/thinkstock.com • Salads p37 © Rohit Seth/iStockphoto/thinkstock • Soups p49 © iStockphoto/thinkstock • Chili p65 © Thomas M Perkins/Hemera/Thinkstock • Dutch Oven p77 © Harry Thomas/istockphoto/thinkstock • Vegetables p89 © Diane Diederich/iStockphoto • Beef p111 © Mike Cherim/iStockphoto/thinkstock • Pork p137 © iStockphoto/thinkstock • Sauces p153 © Brett Mulcahy/Hemera/thinkstock • Poultry p165 © William Berry/Hemera/thinkstock •Fish p181 © Elzbieta Sekowska/Istockphoto/thinkstock • Cookies p195 © iStockphoto/thinkstock • Cakes p213 © iStockphoto/thinkstock.

CONTENTS

INTRODUCTION

Everything is bigger in Texas. Kent and I have heard it since we were children, and we believed it. Researching this cookbook certainly brought that point home as we quickly discovered that when it comes to cooking in the Lone Star State, there's more than just beef on the table.

The pleasures of Texas cooking are as big and bountiful as the state itself. From frontier campfire cooking, to spicy Tex-Mex fare, from old-fashioned cowboy cooking, to the German influence of Central Texas, to southeast Texas' own style of Cajun and Creole cuisine, Texas cooking is diverse... and delicious.

It is our goal to preserve those recipes that have been handed down through generations... favorite recipes from countless family Sunday dinners, recipes that have been cooked on the ranch for years and years, and the recipe your grandmother then your mother then you have made for so many years no one remembers where it actually originated. Some of the best cooks in Texas graciously shared their favorite recipes for this cookbook.

No Texas cookbook would be complete without the Lone Star State's Big Three—barbecue, chili, and Tex-Mex. We bring you ***Cheesy Pork Quesadillas***, ***Chicken Chilaquiles***, ***Texas Red Chili***, and ***Baby Back Ribs with Coffee Bourbon Sauce***. But Texas cooking is more than that. Central Texas brings you the down-home flavor of ***Chicken Fried Steak with White Gravy*** and ***Sweet Potato Pie***. The best cooks in the deep southeast area of Texas bring you the Cajun- and Creole-influenced ***Shrimp Po'Boy with Cajun Confetti Slaw***, ***Meatball Fricasee (Boulette Stew)***, and ***Texas Crawfish Cornbread***. And, of course, you'll enjoy delicious ethnic recipes like ***Ham and Cheese Kolache*** and ***Wurstfest Sausage Cheese Balls***.

Nowhere is the diversity of Texas cooking more evident than during the many festivals that are held throughout the state each year. And throughout this book, you'll enjoy fun stories and pictures about food-related festivals across the state. From Seymour's Fish Day to Texas Rio Grande Valley Onion Festival in Weslaco, from Hot Diggity Hog Fest in Odessa to the Black-Eyed Pea Fest/ October Fest in Athens, there's a celebration to suit every taste.

Our gratitude goes to the many gracious people associated with these festivals. You were helpful and generous with your time and this book is all the better for the assistance you provided. Thank you, too, Tony Smith (and your family of great Texas Cooks) and George Eager (for your Lone Star perspective on good Texas food) and Dana (who is never to be forgotten) and our own hometown sales team, Melissa, Leslie, and Brooke. And, as always, a big thank you goes to Annette Goode (without your support we'd be lost). Last, but always first with us, our love and appreciation goes to our families for their unwavering support; Ally and Macee, Roger, Ryan, and Nicholas—we couldn't do it without you.

We sincerely hope you enjoy using this latest edition of our STATE HOMETOWN COOKBOOK SERIES as much as we enjoyed writing it. When it comes to hometown cooking, Texas is like a whole other country because there is so much great food to enjoy. With our *Texas Hometown Cookbook* we hope to bring you the BEST the Lone Star State has to offer.

Wishing you many happy kitchen memories,

Sheila Simmons & Kent Whitaker

"Let us not become weary in doing good,
for at the proper time we will reap a harvest
if we do not give up"

Galatians 6:9 (NIV)

Appetizers

Tomato Onion Salsa, page 14

Deep-Fried Jalapeños

12 whole jalapeños
½ pound white American cheese, grated
Real Bacon Bits
2 eggs, lightly beaten
½ cup milk

¼ teaspoon salt
⅛ teaspoon Fiesta Brand® Black Pepper
¾ cup all-purpose flour
Oil for deep-frying*

While wearing gloves, cut tops off jalapeños, scoop out seeds and remove stems. In a bowl, combine cheese and bacon bits. Stuff each jalapeno with ½ to 1 tablespoon cheese and bacon mixture. In a separate bowl, combine eggs and milk. In another bowl, mix salt and pepper with flour. Roll filled jalapeños in flour mixture, then in egg mixture, then again in flour mixture. Deep fry in hot oil until golden brown. Do not over-cook or cheese will leak out.

*For a healthier alternative, you can use Texas Pecan Oil.

Fried Pepper Jack Sticks

1 pound pepper jack cheese
3 tablespoons flour
2 eggs
¼ cup each: water and milk
½ cup breadcrumbs
½ cup finely crushed corn chips
⅓ cup grated Parmesan cheese
¼ teaspoon Fiesta Brand® Garlic Powder
Oil for frying*

ISTOCKPHOTO/THINKSTOCK

Cut pepper jack cheese into ½-inch x ½-inch strips (about the size of restaurant-style cheese sticks). Coat each piece evenly with flour; set aside. In a shallow bowl, combine eggs, water and milk. In another bowl, combine breadcrumbs, corn chips, Parmesan and garlic powder. Coat cheese sticks in egg mixture then in crumb mixture; repeat the process. Carefully fry in hot oil until golden (30 to 45 seconds). Cook only a few at a time. Rest on a paper towel to drain; serve hot.

*For a healthier alternative, you can use Texas Pecan Oil instead of oil.

Wurstfest Sausage Cheese Balls

1 pound spicy (hot) sausage, room temperature
1 pound Velveeta cheese, room temperature
1 pound Bisquick (biscuit mix)

Mix ingredients until well blended making sure there are no large pieces of cheese and sausage. After ingredients are well blended, separate portions into pieces about the size of a large tablespoon. Roll portions in balls until smooth. Bake at 325° about 15 minutes or until slightly brown on bottom.

WURSTFEST, NEW BRAUNFELS
REPUBLICAN WOMEN'S WURSTFEST BOOTH

WURSTFEST

Friday before first Monday in November
New Braunfels

Wurstfest is a unique celebration rich in German culture and full of Texas fun. This fun 10-day festival features a variety of entertainment, food and fun on the Wurstfest Grounds in Landa Park and many special events throughout New Braunfels and Comal County. Nestled in the Texas Hill Country, New Braunfels is conveniently located on IH 35 between San Antonio and Austin. The Wurstfest grounds lie just inside Landa Park along the banks of the Comal River.

1.800.221.4369 • www.wurstfest.com

Bacon-Wrapped Wienies

40 hot dogs (wienies)
1 pound bacon
1 (16-ounce) box light brown sugar
Toothpicks

Cut hot dogs in half. Cut bacon strips in thirds. Wrap bacon around hot dogs; secure with toothpicks. Combine brown sugar with enough water to make a saucy consistency. Pour over hot dogs and bake at 350° for 1½ hours. Good to take along in a crockpot. Great for a day at the lake!

SEYMOUR CHAMBER OF COMMERCE

Beer-Battered Onion Rings

1 large Texas Sweet 1015, Vidalia or other sweet onion
1 can beer
3 cups flour, divided
Sea salt

Everyone attending the Fish Day Celebration eventually fries up a mess of catfish. Along with the catfish comes hushpuppies, fried onion rings, and always, always, stuffed jalapeños. I don't know how, but somewhere you can always manage to find a can of beer at the event that you can coax off of someone (donated for the cause), if you promise to share the results!

Slice onion into ½-inch-wide rings. Separate rings. Combine beer and 2 cups flour in a gallon zip-lock bag mixing well to make a semi-thick paste. (More beer or flour may be added to keep coating consistency.) Dip onion rings into beer-batter covering onion well. Gently drop coated onion rings into a Dutch oven or equivalent pot or fryer with at least 3 inches hot oil. When rings turn light brown on one side, turn over to brown lightly on other side. Lightly season with sea salt immediately after removing from fryer. Mound onion rings on platter and enjoy (if there are any left from the chefs)!

MYRA BUSBY, SEYMOUR CHAMBER OF COMMERCE

Tomato Onion Salsa

3 cans diced tomatoes
1 cup finely diced red onion
¼ cup red wine vinegar
2 jalapeño peppers, seeded and minced
½ cup chopped fresh cilantro
1 tablespoon Fiesta Brand® Chili Powder
½ teaspoon salt
1 pinch Fiesta Brand® Cayenne Pepper, or to taste

Combine everything in a bowl. Refrigerate before serving.

THREE RIVERS SALSA FESTIVAL
April • Three Rivers

The Three Rivers Salsa Festival celebrates everything salsa including music, food and dancing. The ten-year-old festival features two stages of continuous music, a salsa making competition, salsa eating contest, a bicycle race and about 60 food and arts and crafts booths. This free event, with children's area, attracts about 6,000 people.

1.888.600.3115 • www.threeriverssalsa.com

Salsa

1 pound tomatoes, chopped
5 green chiles, chopped
2 garlic cloves, chopped
1 teaspoon salt
1 cup water
½ cup finely chopped onion
½ cup finely chopped cilantro

Boil first 5 ingredients for 7 minutes. Place in bowl; stir in onion and cilantro. Refrigerate. Serve cold with chips.

SEYMOUR CHAMBER OF COMMERCE

Plum Tomato and Corn Salsa

10 plum tomatoes, chopped
1 onion, chopped
1 jalapeño pepper, seeded and minced
1 small can whole-kernel corn
2 garlic cloves, minced
1 teaspoon cumin powder
2 teaspoons Fiesta Brand® Chili Powder
1 teaspoon salt
Fiesta Brand® Cilantro to taste
2 teaspoons lemon juice

Combine everything in a bowl. Refrigerate before serving.

Salad Shrimp Con Queso

2 pounds frozen salad shrimp, thawed
1 small bell pepper, chopped
1 jalapeño pepper, seeded and chopped
1 small onion, chopped
1 teaspoon minced garlic

½ stick butter*
2 cans cream of mushroom soup
½ to 1 soup can milk
1 can diced tomatoes
2 (1-pound) packages Velveeta cheese, cubed

Rinse shrimp and set aside to completely thaw. In a skillet, sauté bell pepper, jalapeño, onion and garlic in butter. Combine everything, except shrimp, in a large covered pan and cook over low heat until cheese melts. Add shrimp and cook 5 minutes longer. Serve in small bowls with rice and chips on the side or allow to rest to thicken and serve with chips.

*For a healthier alternative, you can use Texas Pecan Oil instead of butter.

Queso Blanco [White Cheese]

1½ cups finely shredded Monterey Jack or asadero cheese
1 can green chiles, not drained
¼ cup half & half
2 tablespoons finely chopped onion
2 teaspoons ground cumin
½ teaspoon salt
1 tablespoon Fiesta Brand® Cilantro

Asadero is a white cow's-milk cheese of Mexican origin that's available in braids, balls, or rounds. Asadero, which means "roaster" or "broiler," has good melting properties and becomes softly stringy when heated—very similar to an unaged Monterey Jack cheese. Asadero is sometimes called Chihuahua or Oaxaca.

Put all ingredients in a double boiler over medium heat. (Or cook on low in a saucepan.) Cook until melted and well blended, stirring occasionally.

Dried Chipotle Chile Dip

4 chipotle chiles
1 can green chiles
1 cup salsa
1 cup sour cream

Chipotle (pronounced chih-POHT-lay) chile is actually a dried, smoke jalapeño. It has a wrinkled, dark brown skin and a smoky, sweet, almost chocolaty flavor.

Remove stems and seeds from dried chiles and place in saucepan. Cover with water and bring to a boil. Remove from heat and soak in cooking water until soft. Remove skin (reserve cooking water) and process in a blender or food processor with 1 tablespoon cooking water (add more water, if needed, to make a thin paste). Combine in a bowl with remaining ingredients. Chill and serve.

Chili Dip

1 can chili without beans or 1 cup homemade chili
½ cup chopped onion
2 teaspoons Fiesta Brand® Garlic Powder
2 teaspoons Fiesta Brand® Chili Powder
3 tablespoons water
1 can stewed tomatoes, undrained
1 can green chiles
Salt and Fiesta Brand® Black Pepper
2 teaspoons hot sauce
½ cup shredded Monterey Jack cheese
1 (8-ounce) package cream cheese

Combine everything in a saucepan and cook over low heat until heated and well mixed. Serve hot with chips.

Texas Caviar

2 cans black-eyed peas, drained
1 can diced tomatoes, drained
2 jalapeños, seeded and minced
1 small onion, diced
½ yellow bell pepper, finely chopped
¼ cup chopped fresh cilantro
6 tablespoons red wine vinegar
6 tablespoons olive oil*
½ teaspoon salt
½ teaspoon Fiesta Brand® Black Pepper
½ teaspoon Fiesta Brand® Garlic Powder
1 teaspoon Fiesta Brand® Oregano
1½ teaspoons ground cumin

Combine everything in a bowl. Refrigerate at least an hour before serving.

*For a healthier alternative, you can use Texas Pecan Oil instead of olive oil.

BLACK-EYED PEA FEST/OCTOBER FEST

Second Saturday in October • Athens

The East Texas Arboretum is a treasure of rolling hills, hiking trails, beautiful gardens, an 1800's historic home, and home of the Black-Eyed Pea Fest. Athens was the largest producer of black-eyed peas in the world and is known as the Black-Eyed Pea Capital of the World. Local farmers still grow the famous "cow pea" and recipes from unique to dessert are enjoyed at the annual Black-Eyed Pea Fest. Scarecrow trails, entertainment, children's cook-off, art show, arts and craft booths are enjoyed by all!

903.675.5630 • www.eastexasarboretum.org

Hot Sausage Hoppin' John Dip

1 pound ground hot breakfast sausage
½ cup finely chopped onion
½ tablespoon minced garlic
1 small red bell pepper, chopped
¾ cup minced cabbage
¾ cup uncooked brown rice
2 cans chicken broth
2 cans black-eyed peas, drained
2 teaspoons hot sauce
Salt and Fiesta Brand® Black Pepper to taste

Brown sausage and drain. Stir in onion, garlic and bell pepper. Stir in remaining ingredients. Cover and simmer 20 minutes or until peas and rice are tender and liquid is absorbed. Serve surrounded by crackers and tortillas.

Black-Eyed Pea Dip

2 cups cooked black-eyed peas or 1 (16-ounce) can black-eyed peas
1 small onion, chopped
1 can diced tomatoes
½ cup grated sharp Cheddar cheese
Dash hot sauce
Salt and Fiesta Brand® Black Pepper to taste
1 teaspoon Fiesta Brand® Cayenne Pepper

Mash peas slightly (but do not cream). Stir in remaining ingredients and mix well. Serve cold or heated.

Guacamole

2 ripe avocados, peeled
2 tablespoons lime or lemon juice
2 tablespoons minced white onion
1 jalapeño pepper, seeded and minced
1 small tomato, chopped and drained

2 tablespoons Fiesta Brand® Cilantro
1 small garlic clove, minced
Dash Fiesta Brand® Chili Powder
½ teaspoon salt
Dash Fiesta Brand® Black Pepper

Mash peeled avocadoes in a bowl. Stir in lime or lemon juice. Add remaining ingredients. Adjust seasonings to taste. Serve immediately.

Layered Avocado Dip

1 can refried beans
1 can green chiles
1 envelope taco seasoning
2 avocados, seeded, peeled and mashed
1 tablespoon lemon juice

2 tablespoons taco sauce
1 cup sour cream
1 tomato, chopped
1 small can sliced black olives
1 cup Monterrey Jack cheese

Combine refried beans, chiles and taco seasoning; spread over bottom of a glass baking dish. Combine mashed avocados, lemon juice and taco sauce; spread over bean mixture. Top with sour cream and sprinkle on chopped tomatoes, olives and cheese. Serve with tortilla chips.

Bread & Breakfast

Cheddar Pepper Bread, page 23

Flour Tortillas

2 cups flour
1 teaspoon baking powder (for fluffy tortillas)
1 teaspoon salt
1 tablespoon vegetable shortening
¾ cups water

Combine flour, baking powder and salt. Add shortening and mix by hand until lumps are gone. Add water, a little at a time, kneading until smooth. Form dough into balls about the size of ping pong balls. Using a rolling pin, or tortilla press, roll each dough ball into about a 6-inch circle. Cook in a hot skillet treated with nonstick spray until set.

Corn Tortillas

The trick to corn tortillas is using the corn flour known as masa harina (not cornmeal).

2 cups instant corn flour (masa harina)
1⅓ cups warm water
Dash salt

Combine corn flour, water and a dash of salt. Mix into a dough. Add water if too dry, more corn flour if too wet. Form dough into balls about the size of ping pong balls. Using a rolling pin, or tortilla press, roll each dough ball into about a 6-inch circle. Cook in a hot skillet treated with a nonstick spray until set.

Masa harina is Spanish for "dough flour" and is a corn flour made from dried masa (sun- or fire-dried corn kernels cooked in limewater, soaked in limewater overnight, and ground).

Cheddar Pepper Bread

2½ cups flour
1 tablespoon baking powder
¼ teaspoon salt
¾ cup milk
½ cup mayonnaise

1 egg, beaten
2 cups shredded Cheddar cheese
1 small onion, minced
2 tablespoons minced jalapeño pepper or canned green chiles

Combine all ingredients and pour into a prepared loaf or cake pan. Bake at 425° for 20 to 25 minutes or until a toothpick inserted near the center comes out clean.

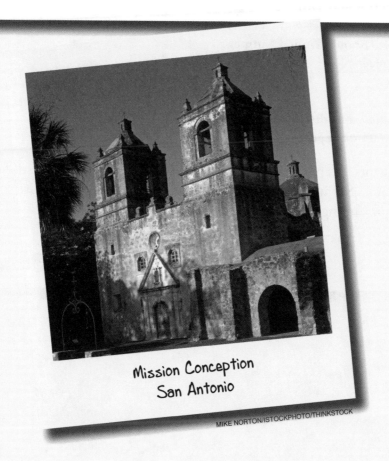

Mission Conception
San Antonio

MIKE NORTON/ISTOCKPHOTO/THINKSTOCK

Yam [Sweet Potato] Bread

2 cups sweet potatoes, cooked and mashed and packed into measuring cup
3 cups sugar
1 cup vegetable oil*
4 large eggs, separated
1½ teaspoons Fiesta Brand® Cinnamon
½ teaspoon Fiesta Brand® Ground Cloves
1½ teaspoons vanilla extract
1 teaspoon Fiesta Brand® Ground Nutmeg
1 teaspoon allspice
1 teaspoon salt
3½ cups flour
2 teaspoons baking soda dissolved in ⅔ cups water
1½ cups nuts (walnuts or pecans)

Mix all ingredients except egg whites and nuts. Beat egg whites until stiff and fold into mixture. Stir in nuts. Bake in loaf pan at 350° for 1 hour. Use small loaf pans for gifts during the holidays.

*For a healthier alternative, you can use Texas Pecan Oil.

SANDRA FITE, GILMER

Crusty Spoon Bread

2 tablespoons butter*
½ cup cornmeal
¾ cup flour
1 tablespoon sugar

½ teaspoon salt
1 tablespoon baking power
1 egg, beaten
1 cup milk

Melt butter in baking dish. Combine remaining ingredients and pour in dish. Bake 45 minutes in 375° oven.

*For a healthier alternative, you can use Texas Pecan Oil instead of butter.

CAJUN FRENCH & MUSIC FEST, ANHALT

Sweet & Spicy Banana Butter

3 large ripe bananas, peeled
1 stick butter, softened*
3 tablespoons lemon juice
½ cup sugar

¼ cup brown sugar
1½ teaspoons hot sauce
½ teaspoon ginger

Mash bananas in a bowl until smooth. Add remaining ingredients and hand mix until smooth and creamy. Chill and serve.

*For a healthier alternative, you can use Texas Pecan Oil instead of butter.

Texas Hot Hushpuppies

2½ cups yellow cornmeal
3 tablespoons hot sauce
1 teaspoon sage
1 teaspoon salt
1 teaspoon Fiesta Brand® Black Pepper
1 teaspoon Fiesta Brand® Cayenne Pepper
1 small onion, minced
1 cup milk
1 egg, beaten
Large dash sugar
Large dash Fiesta Brand® Garlic Powder

Mix everything together and drop by spoonful into a deep fryer at 375°. Fry until golden and drain on a paper towel.

Southern Hushpuppy Championships

Fourth week of September • Lufkin

If you've got the secret ingredient to the most delicious hushpuppy recipe, then join us by celebrating and competing in the "deep fried and delicious" fall culinary event — the Southern Hushpuppy Championships. Hushpuppies come in all shapes, sizes, and flavors and will be judged on taste, originality, and appearance. The competition features all types of teams including family teams, business teams, non-profit organization teams, and teams comprised of children and teenagers. Join us for this fun Southern tradition.

936.634.6305 • www.visitlufkin.com

Hushpuppies

2 cups cornmeal
½ teaspoon salt
3 teaspoons baking powder
¾ cup buttermilk
1 tablespoon sugar
1 tablespoon flour
¼ teaspoon baking soda
1 egg, beaten
½ cup chopped onion
Small can chopped green chiles
1 small jalapeño pepper, finely chopped

Combine all ingredients. Drop by spoonfuls into hot oil in deep fryer. Cook until golden. If you don't like your hushpuppies sweet, omit the sugar.

SEYMOUR CHAMBER OF COMMERCE

Every year, my grandad had a fish fry at our cabin at the lake. Grandad caught the fish and my grandmother made her infamous hushpuppies. All the aunts, uncles, cousins and close friends were invited. Over the years, the recipe has been adapted but the traditional fish fry remains the same. Even fifty years later, a weekend at the lake is not complete without fresh fried catfish and grandmother's hushpuppies. It is just a younger generation grandmother.

Texas Crawfish Cornbread

2 cups self-rising cornmeal
½ teaspoon baking powder
1 teaspoon salt
2 eggs, beaten
½ cup oil*
1 medium onion, finely chopped
1 can cream-style corn
¾ cup grated Cheddar cheese
1 can green chiles
1 pound crawfish meat, chopped

Combine everything in a bowl and pour into a prepared baking dish. Bake at 350° for 35 to 40 minutes or until a toothpick inserted in center comes out clean and top is golden.

*For a healthier alternative, you can use Texas Pecan Oil.

TEXAS CRAWFISH & MUSIC FESTIVAL
April • Old Town Spring

The Texas Crawfish & Music Festival, presented by Houston Press, is held each April in Historic Old Town Spring, Texas. The event, one of the largest and most established crawfish festivals in the South, features live entertainment from some of the top country, blues, zydeco and rock acts on three stages, carnival rides, midway games and activities for kids of all ages along with the best food, crawfish and fixings in the land!

1.800.653.8696
www.texascrawfishfestival.com

Tex-Mex Cornbread

2 cups self-rising yellow cornmeal
¾ teaspoon salt
1 can cream-style corn
1 cup sour cream
½ stick butter, softened*
1 egg, beaten
1 cup shredded Cheddar cheese
1 can chili

Combine everything in a bowl and pour into a prepared baking dish. Bake at 350° for 35 to 40 minutes or until a toothpick inserted in center comes out clean and top is golden.

*For a healthier alternative, you can use Texas Pecan Oil instead of butter.

Black Skillet Cornbread

1¼ cups milk
1 cup cornmeal
1 cup all-purpose flour
4 teaspoons baking powder
¾ teaspoon kosher salt
2 eggs, beaten
¼ cup pecan oil

Preheat oven to 425°. Place 9-inch cast-iron skillet in oven to warm it. Mix milk and cornmeal together in small bowl and let soak for 10 minutes. Sift flour, baking powder and salt together in a mixing bowl. Beat cornmeal mixture and eggs into flour mixture until you have a smooth batter, about 1 minute. Remove skillet from oven. Swish pecan oil in the skillet to coat. Pour batter into the skillet. Bake in preheated oven until a toothpick inserted into the center comes out clean, 18 to 23 minutes. Cut into wedges to serve. Makes 8 servings.

TEXAS PECAN RANCH • WWW.TEXASPECANRANCH.COM

Homemade Yeast Rolls

1 package dry active yeast
1 cup boiled water, cooled to lukewarm
2¼ cups all-purpose flour
3 tablespoons sugar
1 teaspoon salt
1 egg, beaten
2 large tablespoons shortening
Vegetable oil*

Dissolve yeast in 1 cup boiled and cooled water. Combine flour, sugar and salt; mix well. Add yeast water; mix well. Add egg and shortening; mix well. Form into a ball and rub with oil. Place in a large bowl, cover with plastic wrap and allow to rise about 2 hours or until doubled in size. Break dough into 12 equal pieces and form into balls. Place on a greased cookie sheet with space between each and allow to rise again. Bake in a preheated 425° oven about 15 minutes or until golden brown.

*For a healthier alternative, you can use Texas Pecan Oil.

Czech Kolache Klobase Festival

Second Saturday in June • East Bernard

This festival began in 1990 and brings people together to enjoy good music, good food and to celebrate ethnic heritage and culture. Plenty of music, dancing, lively polka entertainment with bands, entertainers, dancers. Arts, crafts, home cooked bbq chicken/sausage plate lunch for sale, cake walk, children's entertainment and plenty of kolaches for sale. Located at air conditioned Riverside Hall with large wooden dance floor with an adjacent outdoor water-fan cooled pavilion.

979.335.7907 • www.kkfest.com

Ham and Cheese Kolache

Ham and Cheese Filling:

1 cup diced ham
½ cup shredded Swiss cheese

¼ cup grated Parmesan cheese
2 tablespoons Dijon mustard

Kolache Dough:

3 to 3½ cups all-purpose flour, divided
¼ cup grated Parmesan cheese
1 tablespoon sugar
1 envelope fast-rising yeast
1 teaspoon salt

1 cup plus 1 tablespoon water, divided
2 tablespoons butter or margarine*
1 large egg
1 egg white
1 tablespoon water

Combine all filling ingredients; mix well. Refrigerate. In a large bowl, combine 1 cup flour, cheese, sugar, undissolved yeast and salt. Heat 1 cup water and butter until very warm (120° to 130°); gradually add to flour mixture. Beat 2 minutes at medium speed of electric mixer, scraping bowl occasionally. Add egg and another 1 cup flour; beat 2 minutes at high speed. Stir in enough remaining flour to make a soft dough. Knead on lightly floured surface until smooth and elastic, about 8 to 10 minutes. Cover; let rest 10 minutes. Divide dough into 16 equal pieces; shape each into a ball. Cover; let rest 15 minutes. Place balls 2 inches apart on greased baking sheets. Make a deep and wide indentation on each ball by pushing outward toward edge, leaving ½-inch ridge around outside. Fill with ham and cheese filling. Cover and let rise until doubled in size, about 1 hour. Brush surface with a mixture of 1 egg white and 1 tablespoon water. Bake at 375° for 15 minutes or until done. Serve warm.

*For a healthier alternative, you can use Texas Pecan Oil instead of butter.

Breakfast Biscuits

2 cups all-purpose flour
2½ teaspoons baking powder
½ teaspoon salt
⅓ cup shortening
¾ cup milk

Sift together flour, baking powder and salt. Cut in shortening with fork until mixture resembles coarse meal. Add milk and mix with fork until flour is moistened and dough pulls away from sides of bowl. Turn out on lightly floured board. Knead and roll ¾-inch thick. Cut with a biscuit cutter, and place on lightly greased pan. Bake at 450° for 12 to 15 minutes.

Jalapeno Spoon Biscuits

2½ cups self-rising flour
2 tablespoons mayonnaise
1¼ cups milk
1 tablespoon sugar
3 tablespoons minced jalapeño pepper
½ cup finely shredded Cheddar cheese

Combine all ingredients in a small bowl. Drop by teaspoon onto a nonstick cookie sheet. Bake at 450° for 12 to 15 minutes, or until golden brown.

Layered Herb Crepes

Crepes:

2 cups all-purpose flour
4 eggs
2 cups milk
½ cup finely chopped parsley

4 tablespoons chopped basil
4 tablespoons chopped dill
Lemon Sauce
Chive Butter

Put flour and eggs in bowl, whisk in enough milk to make a smooth batter the consistency of thick whipping cream. If there are lumps in batter, strain into another jug before making crepes. Heat frying pan with small amount of butter (or spray with cooking spray) until hot. Add a small amount of batter and swirl around pan until covered, adding more if needed or pouring out excess if too much. Cook until crêpe is lightly golden on bottom, turn over and cook other side for a few seconds. These can be made in advance and frozen (with plastic wrap or wax paper between each one). Spread 1 crêpe with Chive Butter, stack another on top and spread with Chive Butter. Continue layering with remaining crêpes and Chive Butter. Place in oven proof dish and bake in 300° oven about 10 minutes. Cut into wedges and serve with Lemon Sauce.

Chive Butter:

1 stick butter, softened
2 tablespoons chopped fresh chives

2 teaspoons French Dijon mustard
½ teaspoon grated lemon rind

Mix all ingredients well. This can be made a day or two earlier and refrigerated.

Lemon Sauce:

2 ounces (½ stick) butter*
1 tablespoon all-purpose flour
1¼ cups chicken stock

1 egg yolk
1 tablespoon lemon juice
1 tablespoon chopped parsley

Melt butter in small pot; stir in flour. Cook and stir 1 minute. Gradually stir in stock until sauce boils and thickens. Reduce heat; quickly stir in egg yolk, lemon juice and parsley. Reheat.

*For a healthier alternative, you can use Texas Pecan Oil instead of butter.

THE MAIN COURSE, PLANO (WWW.MAINCOURSECOOKING.COM)

Banana Nut Waffles

1⅓ cups all-purpose flour
1 teaspoon baking soda
2 teaspoons baking powder
2 teaspoons sugar
¼ teaspoon salt
3 eggs
1½ teaspoons vanilla extract
1⅓ cups milk
⅓ cup melted butter*
2 bananas, mashed
½ cup pecans
Dash Fiesta Brand® Cinnamon

Banana Nut Waffles truly hit the spot for a quick breakfast on the go. You can make this the night before and eat them cold at the lake or heat them up on the BBQ grill along with the syrup.

Combine flour, baking soda, baking powder, sugar and salt in a bowl; set aside. Whisk together eggs, vanilla extract and milk in a separate bowl. Stir in melted butter and flour mixture until a slightly lumpy batter forms. Add bananas, pecans and a dash of cinnamon. Cook in preheated waffle iron until steam stops coming out of the seam, about 2 minutes. Serve with your favorite brand maple syrup (heated).

Note: Don't have time for home-made waffles? Use your favorite pancake mix following waffle recipe on box and then add bananas, pecans, and cinnamon.

*For a healthier alternative, you can use Texas Pecan Oil instead of butter.

SEYMOUR CHAMBER OF COMMERCE

Texas French Toast

12 slices Texas toast
4 eggs
1½ cups milk
2 teaspoons vanilla coffee creamer

1½ tablespoons brown sugar
1 cup chopped pecans, divided
Powdered Sugar

Combine eggs, milk, creamer, brown sugar and ½ cup pecans in a large bowl. Dip each piece of toast into egg mixture. Cook on a hot skillet until golden brown. Remove from skillet and sprinkle with reserved pecans. Serve hot sprinkled with powdered sugar.

Fried Peppers & Eggs on Texas Toast

Oil*
4 teaspoons minced jalapeño, divided
4 eggs, divided
Fiesta Brand® Black Pepper

Fiesta Brand® Chili Powder
2 tablespoons butter, softened*
4 slices Texas Toast

Heat oil in a skillet, and make a pile of 1 teaspoon jalapeño. Quickly crack 1 egg on top of jalapeño and season with black pepper and chili powder to taste. Flip egg to cook on other side. When ready, serve hot on a slice of buttered toasted Texas Toast. Repeat with remaining ingredients.

*For a healthier alternative, you can use Texas Pecan Oil.

SHAUN EDMONDS, HOUSTON

"Gas House" Eggs

Sliced Bread (enough to feed everyone)
Butter*
Fiesta Brand® Garlic Powder
Fiesta Brand® Seasoning Salt
Eggs (one egg for each slice of bread)

Gary Dozier of Crowley says, "My Dad made this and my brother and son carry on the tradition. Everyone asks why it's called 'Gas House' Eggs. Before fast food restaurants, there were service stations (or gas houses) with a hot griddle and a cook who could check under the hood, fill the tank and whip up a quick breakfast. This is one that always brings the late risers to the kitchen."

Cut or pinch a hole in the center of a piece of sliced bread. Heat skillet melting several pats of butter. Add garlic powder and seasoning salt to butter. Add bread to skillet and turn coating both sides. Crack and place an egg directly in hole in center of bread. When egg is cooked on one side, flip bread quickly and carefully. Remove when eggs is cooked on other side. The result is a quick flavorful breakfast contained in one compact package.

*For a healthier alternative, you can use Texas Pecan Oil instead of butter.

GARY DOZIER, CROWLEY

Hash Brown Green Chile Casserole

1 bag frozen hash browns, thawed
6 eggs, beaten
2 cans green chiles, drained
1 stick butter, melted*
1 pound browned ground sausage
1 cup shredded cheese
1 can cream mushroom soup
1 small onion, chopped
Salt and Fiesta Brand® Black Pepper to taste

Combine everything in a large bowl, and place in a greased baking dish. Bake at 350° about 45 minutes.

*For a healthier alternative, you can use Texas Pecan Oil instead of butter.

Salads

Mom's Potato Salad, page 44

DESERT CREEK HONEY

Raw Honey Spreads

What's all the buzz about? Desert Creek creamed honeys are:

• Sustainable • Artisanal • Produced with absolute transparency • Fresh • Nutritious

Desert Creek Honey was founded in 2003 by 13-year-old Blake Shook. Blake is still the CEO of Desert Creek Honey, where every drop of honey sold is produced and packaged by Desert Creek. This gives them a very unique position of control over every aspect of the production and quality of every product sold. Based just outside of Dallas, Texas, they are a true Texas company, selling local Texas honey.

Six simplistic spreads have countless everyday uses:

- Drizzled over granola, cereal or yogurt
- Glazed on meats or mixed with marinades
- Spread on toast, bagels, biscuits or rolls
- Warmed and poured over ice cream
- Mixed with hot teas or coffee

www.desertcreekhoney.com
214-886-6899
blake@desertcreekhoney.com

Honey Garden Salad

4 cups mixed salad greens
1/4 cup chopped pecans or pine nuts
1/4 cup raisins
1/2 cup berry-flavored or balsamic
    vinegar

1/4 cup honey
1 to 2 tablespoons olive oil*
2 tablespoons Italian dressing
1 cup mixed fruit, drained

Combine everything in a bowl and toss to coat greens.

*For a healthier alternative, you can use Texas Pecan Oil instead of olive oil.

Honey Mustard Salad

Bag spinach leaves
2 carrots, chopped
1 cup broccoli pieces
1/2 cup chopped onion
1 cup mayonnaise

3 tablespoons orange juice
1 tablespoon half-and-half
3 tablespoons Dijon mustard
2 tablespoons honey

Combine spinach, carrots, broccoli and onion; mix well. Combine remaining ingredients adding a bit of oil or water to thin if needed. Toss with salad and chill before serving.

Fresco Strawberry Salad

1 bag leaf spinach
1 cup chopped pecans
½ cup bacon bits
1 cup chopped strawberries
1 cup crumbled queso fresco cheese
½ cup chopped red onion
Bottled raspberry vinaigrette to taste
Handful of raisins (optional)
Dash salt and Fiesta Brand® Black Pepper

Place all ingredients in a serving bowl and toss.

Queso fresco is a white, slightly salty fresh Mexican cheese with a texture similar to farmer cheese. It is available in cottage cheese-style tubs in Latin American markets and from many supermarkets. Also called queso blanco.

PASADENA STRAWBERRY FESTIVAL
Third weekend in May • Pasadena

The Pasadena Strawberry Festival is a three-day event and one of the largest and most popular annual events in the Pasadena area. This award-winning event offers a wide variety of both indoor and outdoor activities, attractions and entertainment ranging from the "World's Largest Strawberry Shortcake", barbecue cookoffs and helicopter rides to continuous musical entertainment, children's activities and the State Mud Volleyball Championship Tournament—a fun-filled weekend of activities for the whole family to enjoy.

281.991.9500 • www.strawberryfest.org

Bean Salad

1 can kidney beans, drained and rinsed
2 cans cut green beans, drained
1 can wax beans, drained
1 can whole-kernel corn, drained
2 celery stalks, finely chopped
1 green bell pepper, chopped
1 red bell pepper, chopped
½ cup sliced olives
½ cup chopped onion
1 tablespoon vinegar
4 tablespoons salad oil*
Salt, Fiesta Brand® Black Pepper and favorite salad dressing to taste

Combine all ingredients in a bowl; stir.

*For a healthier alternative, you can use Texas Pecan Oil.

Cilantro Lime Pasta Salad

Dressing:

1 cup fresh cilantro
⅓ cup Pecan Oil
½ cup plain yogurt
1 (4-ounce) can roasted mild green chilies
2 cloves garlic, roughly chopped
1 teaspoon cumin
¾ teaspoon kosher salt
Zest of 1 lime

Layer Dressing ingredients in blender and blend until smooth.

Salad:

4 cups cooked pasta, cold
2 cups summer veggies (grape tomatoes, red onions, red peppers), sliced or chopped
1 (15-ounce) can black beans, drained
1 (15-ounce) can sweet corn
¼ cup chopped fresh basil and cilantro

Toss Salad ingredients and dressing together and chill (or eat it right away).

Variation: Add grilled, sliced chicken breast.

TEXAS PECAN RANCH • WWW.TEXASPECANRANCH.COM

Cornbread Salad

1 box cornbread mix plus ingredients to prepare per directions on box
  (or homemade cornbread)
1 can pinto beans, drained and rinsed
1 large sweet onion, chopped
1 can whole-kernel corn
1 can diced tomatoes and chiles, drained
Bottled ranch dressing
1 cup shredded Cheddar cheese
½ cup Real Bacon Bits

I fell in love with this dish during a trip along the Texas coast.

Make your favorite cornbread recipe from a box or from your recipe; set aside to cool. Combine remaining ingredients with ranch dressing to taste. Crumble cornbread and stir into salad gently. Add more dressing, as needed, until ingredients are coated well, stirring gently to prevent crushing cornbread. Cover and chill an hour or longer before serving.

Honey Ranch Broccoli Salad

4 cups broccoli florets
½ cup bacon bits
1 carrot, diced
½ cup chopped celery
Dash Fiesta Brand® Garlic Powder

Dash Fiesta Brand® Crushed Red Pepper
1 tablespoon honey
Ranch dressing to taste
Croutons

Combine all ingredients, except croutons, in a bowl and toss. Chill and serve topped with croutons.

Avocado Cucumber Salad

2 medium cucumbers, cubed
2 avocados, cubed
4 tablespoons chopped fresh cilantro
1 garlic clove, minced
2 tablespoons minced green onions
¼ teaspoon salt
Fiesta Brand® Black Pepper to taste
¼ large lemon
1 lime
Flavored croutons to taste

Combine first 7 ingredients. Mix well, cover and chill before serving. Just before serving, drizzle with lemon and lime juice; add croutons and toss.

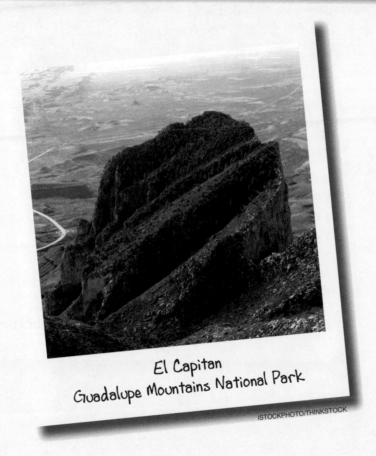

El Capitan
Guadalupe Mountains National Park

ISTOCKPHOTO/THINKSTOCK

Texas Hot Slaw

½ head cabbage, chopped
2 carrots, diced
1 medium onion, chopped
1 red bell pepper, diced
1 chili pepper, minced
1 cup mayonnaise

1 tablespoon sugar
1 tablespoon vinegar
1 teaspoon Fiesta Brand® Black Pepper
½ teaspoon Fiesta Brand® Garlic Powder
Dash Fiesta Brand® Chili Powder
½ tablespoon mustard

Combine everything in a bowl, mix well and chill before serving.

Creamy Classic Coleslaw

½ head cabbage, chopped or shredded
1 large carrot, chopped
1 small onion, finely chopped
1½ cups mayonnaise
2 tablespoons sugar
3 tablespoons vinegar
½ teaspoon salt

Combine everything in a bowl, mix well and chill before serving.

Mom's Potato Salad

6 medium potatoes
2 teaspoons salt (or to taste)
2 eggs, boiled and chopped
1 tablespoon dried onion
½ cup sweet relish
½ cup sliced black olives, optional
1 small jar red pimentos
1 cup mayonnaise (or to taste)
2 tablespoons parsley

Wash and boil potatoes, with skins, about 30 minutes or just until cooked through; cool. When potatoes are cool enough to handle, peel and cut into ½-inch cubes. Add remaining ingredients. Serve immediately.

PAULETTE GOODMAN, JEFFERSON

Hot Mustard Potato Salad

3 pounds red potatoes, rinsed and quartered
⅓ cup mayonnaise
⅓ cup jalapeño mustard
⅓ cup sour cream
½ teaspoon Fiesta Brand® Cajun-All
½ teaspoon Fiesta Brand® Chili Powder
½ teaspoon sugar
1½ cups diced tomatoes
½ cup crumbled cooked bacon
2 tablespoons thinly sliced green onion
Sunflower seeds, almonds or pecans, optional

Place potatoes in large boiler with salted water to cover. Bring to boil over high heat. Reduce heat and cook about 20 minutes or until potatoes are just cooked through (do not overcook). Combine mayonnaise, jalapeño mustard, sour cream, Cajun seasoning, chili powder and sugar in large bowl until well blended. Add warm potatoes; gently stir to coat well. Add tomatoes, bacon and green onions; toss lightly. Chill before serving. Just before serving, gently stir in sunflower seeds, chopped almonds or chopped pecans, if desired.

Taco Chicken Salad

1 (1-pound) head lettuce, chopped
1 teaspoon Fiesta Brand® Chili Powder
1 jar medium salsa
Ranch salad dressing to taste
1 cup shredded Cheddar cheese
¼ cup shredded Monterey Jack cheese

¼ cup chopped black olives
2 carrots, sliced like chips
2 to 3 boneless skinless chicken breasts, fully
    cooked, browned and sliced
1 cup crushed tortilla chips

Place chopped lettuce in a large bowl. Add chili powder, salsa and ranch dressing to taste; toss well. Add both cheeses, olives and carrots; mix gently. Top with chicken slices and crushed tortillas. Serve immediately.

East Texas Poultry Festival

October • Center

There will be food booths, arts and crafts booths, live entertainment, 3-day carnival, cheer competition, poultry judging and auction, art, photography and quilt show and more.

1.800.854.5328
www.shelbycountychamber.com

ROBERT LINTON/ISTOCKPHOTO/THINKSTOCK

Margaret's Chicken Salad

1 medium apple, cored and cut into
    bite-sized pieces
2 cups chicken breasts (boiled,
    deboned and cut into bite-sized
    pieces)
1½ cups halved red seedless grapes

½ cup chopped walnuts
½ cup sliced celery
½ teaspoon crushed dried tarragon
¼ cup chopped fresh parsley
4 to 8 tablespoons mayonnaise

Combine all ingredients; mix well. Serve on lettuce leaves.

SHELBY COUNTY
CHAMBER OF COMMERCE, CENTER

Seared Tex-Mex Chunky Beef Salad

1½ pounds stew meat
Oil or butter*
½ teaspoon Fiesta Brand® Crushed Red
   Pepper
3 garlic cloves, minced
¼ cup lime juice
2 tablespoons red wine

1 red bell pepper, chopped
1 red onion, chopped
2 teaspoons cumin powder
½ tablespoon Fiesta Brand® Cilantro
1 small can whole-kernel corn
1 can diced tomatoes
Salt and Fiesta Brand® Black Pepper

In a large nonstick or cast-iron skillet, sear stew meat in oil or butter. Add red pepper, garlic, lime juice, wine, bell pepper, onion, cumin and cilantro. When meat is done, remove meat only from skillet and place on a platter of salad greens. Stir corn, tomatoes, salt and pepper into skillet with cooked onions and peppers. Stir to mix into a thick, seared salsa. Pour over meat and salad. Serve hot.

*For a healthier alternative, you can use Texas Pecan Oil.

Roquefort Dressing

6 gallons Kraft mayonnaise
1 cup lemon juice
5 ounces M.S.G.
1 gallon whole milk
¼ cup salt

¼ cup white pepper
3 pounds (½ wheel) Roquefort cheese,
   crumbled
10 pounds Blue cheese, crumbled
1 ounce egg-shade food coloring

Combine mayonnaise, lemon juice, M.S.G, milk, salt and pepper; mix well until smooth. Add cheeses and mix slowly to retain chunks. Add in the egg color last and gently stir well. Cover, label with time and date, store in cooler until needed. Makes 8½ gallons. Keeps 4 days in cooler.

BIG TEXAN STEAK RANCH • WWW.BIGTEXAN.COM

Soups, Stews & Chowders

Meatball Fricassee (Boulette Stew), page 52

Chicken Parmesan Soup and Seasoned Oyster Crackers

2 tablespoons Fiesta Brand® Ground Italian Spice Blend (Italian seasoning)
3 chickens, cooked and chunked
3 cartons half and half
7 zucchini, shredded
3 bags Rigatoni noodles, cooked
3 cans/jars sliced mushrooms
1 bag carrots, shredded
2 boxes Parmesan cheese (I prefer the refrigerated kind)
3 cans diced tomatoes

Serves a crowd! The chamber has served this at our Christmas tour of homes.

Heat all ingredients; add water as needed. Serves 70. Serve with seasoned oyster crackers.

Seasoned Oyster Crackers:

1 package oyster crackers
1 cup oil*
1 package Hidden Valley Ranch Homestyle Onion Dressing
1 teaspoon dill
1 teaspoon Fiesta Brand® Garlic Powder

Place crackers in a gallon zip-lock bag. Combine remaining ingredients; add to bag. Toss until crackers absorb oil. Spread on a cookie sheet and bake at 350° until crispy. Cool. Pour back into baggy to transport or freeze.

*For a healthier alternative, you can use Texas Pecan Oil.

SEYMOUR CHAMBER OF COMMERCE

Chilled Pea Soup with Minted Mascarpone

Pea Soup:

2 cups chicken broth
1 garlic clove
5 cups (24 ounces) frozen peas
½ cup heavy cream
½ cup milk
¼ teaspoon salt or to taste
¼ teaspoon Fiesta Brand® White Pepper or to taste

Pour chicken broth into a medium saucepan. Add garlic. Bring to a boil over medium heat and cook several minutes. Remove broth from heat, add frozen peas, and mix well. Set aside a few minutes to allow peas to thaw. Pour into a blender and purée until soup is smooth. Pour broth back into saucepan, add cream and milk, and bring to a simmer over low heat. Simmer 5 minutes; season with salt and pepper. Remove from heat and cool to room temperature. Pour soup into a large bowl, cover with plastic wrap, and chill in refrigerator at least 3 hours.

Minted Mascarpone:

½ cup cream, cold
½ cup (4 ounces) mascarpone, cold
12 fresh mint leaves (6 minced; 6 whole for garnish)

Whip cream using a whisk or electric mixer. Stir in mascarpone. Just before serving, stir in minced mint. To serve, ladle soup into glass tumblers or flat soup bowls and garnish each with a dollop of Minted Mascarpone with a mint leaf in center. Serves 6. (Can also be served warm.)

RECIPE BY PAULA LAMBERT, CHEESE, GLORIOUS CHEESE
SUBMITTED BY GRAPEFEST

Meatball Fricassee [Boulette Stew]

6 heaping tablespoons roux (flour browned in a little oil*)
2 quarts water
1 large onion, chopped
1 small bell pepper, chopped
1 garlic clove, minced
2 pounds ground beef, seasoned to taste
   and made into small balls
Salt, Fiesta Brand® Crushed Red Pepper and
   Fiesta Brand® Black Pepper to taste
½ cup chopped green onions

Dissolve roux in water in a heavy pot over medium heat. (Watch pot closely because roux in water can boil over quickly. What a mess!) Add onions, bell pepper and garlic; bring to a boil. Lower heat and drop meatballs into mixture. Cook until meat is tender. Add green onions about 10 minutes before meat is cooked. Serve over cooked rice or mashed potatoes.

Note: Chopped potatoes and carrots may be added to this stew when the meat is added.

*For a healthier alternative, you can use Texas Pecan Oil.

DAVE DAVENPORT
CAJUN FRENCH MUSIC & FOOD FEST

CAJUN FRENCH MUSIC & FOOD FEST
May • San Antonio

Cajun French Music Association De Fa Tras Chapter presents the Cajun French Music & Food Fest. Join us at Anhalt Hall and enjoy three Cajun bands, dance lessons on the big wooden floor at Anhalt Hall plus great Cajun food.

www.defatrascajun.com

Tex-Mex 15-Minute Albondigas Soup

1 package fully-cooked beef meatballs
2 (14-ounce) cans ready-to-serve beef broth
2 cups frozen corn
1 cup salsa
Tortilla chips, optional
Fiesta Brand® Cilantro, optional

Microwave meatballs according to package directions. Combine beef broth, corn and salsa in medium saucepan. Bring to a boil, and simmer 5 minutes. Add meatballs and serve. Garnish with crumbled tortilla chips and/or chopped cilantro, if desired.

THE TEXAS BEEF COUNCIL

Tex-Mex Cabbage Soup

1½ pounds ground beef browned
1 small onion, finely chopped
2 cans stewed tomatoes
1 small head cabbage, shredded
2 large carrots, sliced
1 package taco seasoning
1 medium can dark red kidney beans
7 cups water

This is a great starter recipe. You can add all kinds of things, corn, additional veggies even chopped smoked sausage!

Brown hamburger meat; drain. Combine all ingredients in a large pot and cook for 1 hour. Stir as needed and serve hot.

Mom's Potato Soup

4 medium potatoes
1 teaspoon McKay's Chicken Seasoning
Salt and Fiesta Brand® Black Pepper to taste
2 cups water
1 can cream of chicken soup

Peel and dice potatoes; cook in seasoned water over medium heat until tender (usually 30 minutes or less). Break with fork until most lumps are gone. Add soup. Adjust seasonings to taste. If too thick, add water. Simmer over low heat about 15 minutes. Serve hot.

PAULETTE GOODMAN, BORN AND RAISED IN JEFFERSON

Black Bean Salsa Soup with Chili Sour Cream

2 cans black beans, drained and rinsed
2 cups water
2 beef bouillon cubes

2 cups chunky salsa
1 teaspoon ground cumin
Dash lemon juice

Chili Sour Cream:

5 tablespoons sour cream
2 tablespoons thinly-sliced green onion

2 teaspoons Fiesta Brand® Chili Powder
1 teaspoon parsley

In a food processor or blender, combine beans, water, bouillon, salsa, cumin and lemon juice. Blend quickly but do not purée (leave it chunky). Pour soup into saucepan and heat over medium heat about 10 to 15 minutes. In a small bowl, combine all Chili Sour Cream ingredients; mix well and chill. Serve Black Bean Salsa Soup in bowls topped with Chili Sour Cream.

Texas Pecan Soup

2 cups pecan halves
6 cups beef broth
1 stick butter*
2 tablespoons finely chopped green onion
1 garlic clove, pressed
2 tablespoons puréed tomato
1 tablespoon cornstarch dissolved in ¼ cup water
1 egg yolk
½ cup cream
½ teaspoon salt
¼ teaspoon Fiesta Brand® White Pepper
1 teaspoon Fiesta Brand® Ground Nutmeg

Grind pecans with broth in blender. Melt butter in large saucepan, add onions and cook 5 minutes over medium heat until soft. Add garlic and cook 1 minute. Slowly add nut/broth mixture, tomato purée and cornstarch. Cook 30 minutes, uncovered, over low heat. Beat egg yolk into cream and slowly whisk into soup; do not boil after this point. Season with salt, pepper and nutmeg.

*For a healthier alternative, you can use Texas Pecan Oil instead of butter.

TEXAS PECAN GROWERS ASSOCIATION

Tomato Soup

1 tablespoon butter*
2 tablespoons minced onion
½ tablespoon minced garlic
4 cups milk
½ teaspoon baking soda

½ teaspoon salt
1 large can tomatoes
1 teaspoon Fiesta Brand® Cilantro
1 teaspoon Fiesta Brand® Chili Powder

In a large pot, cook onion and garlic in butter until golden. Add remaining ingredients and cook about 30 minutes. Break tomatoes up with a fork or spoon for a chunky version or allow soup to cool and use a blender to purée. Reheat and serve.

*For a healthier alternative, you can use Texas Pecan Oil instead of butter.

TOMATO FESTIVAL

June • Jacksonville

Enjoy many tomato activities, including Hot Sauce Contest, gospel concert, karaoke contest, talent contest, lots of kid's activities and much more! Arts/crafts, street dance, and live entertainment add to this family event.

1.800.376.2217
www.jacksonvilletexas.com

Easy Steak and Mushroom Soup Stew

2 pounds cubed stew meat
¼ onion, minced
1 tablespoon minced garlic
2 tablespoons olive oil*
Salt and Fiesta Brand® Black Pepper

3 cups potatoes, cubed
3 cups carrots, chopped
2 cans chopped mushrooms
2 cans cream of mushroom soup
1 envelope dry onion soup mix

Brown stew meat, onions and garlic in olive oil in a large pot. Add remaining ingredients and about 1 cup water. Cover pot and simmer over low heat until veggies are tender. Serve hot.

*For a healthier alternative, you can use Texas Pecan Oil instead of olive oil.

Beef Stew

1 pound cubed stew meat
½ tablespoon cumin powder
Salt and Fiesta Brand® Black Pepper to taste
1 package onion soup mix
6 to 7 potatoes, diced
6 to 7 carrots, chopped

3 celery stalks, finely chopped
2 small onions, chopped
1 green bell pepper, chopped
1 can tomato soup
1½ cups water

Brown stew meat in a skillet with a bit of oil; season with cumin powder, salt and pepper. Combine all ingredients in a pot and cook over medium-high heat. Add additional water as needed or a bit of flour to thicken.

Carne Guisada

3 tablespoons canola oil*
2 pounds beef bottom round steak, cut in 1-inch cubes
2 tablespoons all-purpose (plain) flour
½ green bell pepper, seeded and finely chopped
½ yellow onion, finely chopped
1 large tomato, finely chopped (reserve as much juice as you can)
1 fresh jalapeño pepper, thinly sliced crosswise
3 garlic cloves, finely chopped
½ teaspoon ground cumin
1 teaspoon Fiesta Brand® Chili Powder
½ teaspoon salt
¼ teaspoon freshly ground Fiesta Brand® Black Pepper
½ cup beef stock, water or beer, as needed

In a heavy pot or, preferably, a well-seasoned cast iron Dutch oven, warm canola oil over a medium high heat. Carefully add beef cubes to hot oil and sauté until lightly browned (about 10 minutes). Next, sprinkle flour over browned beef cubes and stir to coat evenly. Cook another minute or 2 to brown flour; add bell pepper, onion, and tomato with juice. Give it all a good stir and mix in jalapeño, garlic, cumin, chili powder, salt and pepper and beef stock, water or beer. (About the stock: I usually use ¼ cup beef stock and ¼ cup beer. Why? It's a great excuse to drink a beer!) Now turn your heat way down low, till the pot just barely bubbles, and simmer until the beef is fork tender (usually about 2½ hours). Check it occasionally to make sure it doesn't stick to the bottom of the pot. If it begins to stick, crack open another cerveza (beer), add a little to pot and then pour the rest down the throat of the chef!

*For a healthier alternative, you can use Texas Pecan Oil.

TONY SMITH, BORN IN JEFFERSON

Carne Guisada is a simple beef stew popular in south Texas around San Antonio and all long both sides of the Rio Grande. It is most often served with refried beans, creamy guacamole and hot homemade flour tortillas. It's also great with a good biscuit and if my Aunt Gladys was still alive, I'd walk five miles in the hot Texas sun for a bowl of Carne Guisada served up with one of her monster cathead biscuits. Carne Guisada is always best the day after you cook it, especially for breakfast. In south Texas border towns like Brownsville, Reynosa, Piedra Negras, Laredo, Del Rio and Eagle Pass, it is common to find it served piping hot and wrapped in a fresh flour tortilla for a handy first meal of the day. Serving Carne Guisada the next day, gives all the juices, root vegetables and spices time to meld with the beef. Chances are you won't be able wait that long, however. In that case, serve it hot from the pot in warmed ceramic bowls. Garnish with fresh jalapeño slices and set it beside some pinto or refried beans, guacamole, tomato slices and sour cream. A frosty Dr. Pepper bottled in Dublin boosts this south Texas fare into culinary Nirvana. I'm not exactly sure where that's at, but I think it's just down the road from Happy.

— Tony Smith was born in Jefferson, Texas and currently lives in Chattanooga, Tennessee. When friends remind him that Tennesseans are nicknamed Volunteers because they went to Texas to fight Generalissimo Antonio de Padua María Severino López de Santa Anna y Pérez de Lebrón, he reminds them that Texans can afford to hire whomever they choose!

Trail Master Stew

2 pounds ground beef, browned
2 cans red kidney beans
2 cans stewed tomatoes
1 can whole-kernel corn
1 chili pepper, chopped
1 small onion, chopped
Salt and Fiesta Brand® Black Pepper to taste
2 tablespoons Worcestershire sauce

Combine all; add water to desired consistency. Simmer at least 1 hour.

Minced Jalapeno Beef Stew

2 pounds stew meat (beef or goat)
Oil*
4 tablespoons minced jalapeño peppers with 1 tablespoon juice from jar
2 carrots, diced
3 cups diced potatoes
1 onion, chopped
1 bottle Shiner Bach or favorite beer
1 can beef stock
1 can diced tomatoes
1 can whole-kernel corn
1 cup water
2 tablespoons cornmeal

Brown meat in oil; drain excess grease and stir in jalapeños just long enough to brown edges. Combine with remaining ingredients in a large pot and cook, covered, until potatoes are tender.

*For a healthier alternative, you can use Texas Pecan Oil.

Posole

2½ pounds pork, cubed
1 onion, chopped
3 garlic cloves, minced
2 tablespoons oil*
4 cans chicken broth
1 can beef broth
4 cans water

2 teaspoons Fiesta Brand® Oregano
2 teaspoons salt
3 tablespoons Fiesta Brand® Chili Powder
3 cans white hominy, drained
1 teaspoon Fiesta Brand® Cilantro
1 teaspoon cumin powder

Toppings:

Sliced radishes
Sliced onions

Lime wedges
Cheese

Brown pork, onions and garlic in oil. Combine with remaining ingredients in a large pot. Simmer covered about 3 hours on low. Serve hot over rice with topping items as desired.

*For a healthier alternative, you can use Texas Pecan Oil.

TEXAS RICE FESTIVAL

First Weekend of October • Winnie

The first Texas Rice Festival was held in downtown Winnie in 1969. It is now a week-long event featuring a carnival, parades, livestock show, open horse show, BBQ cook-off, nightly street dances, antique car show, cooking contest, pageants, karaoke, and features food made with rice and featuring the flavors of the Cajun culture which is strong in the area. Typical fare includes rice balls, gumbo, étouffée, pistolettes, blooming onions, crab balls, boudin balls, funnel cakes and many other delicacies. The event is renowned for its outstanding cuisine.

409.296.4404 • www.texasricefestival.org

SF_FOODPHOTO/ ISTOCKPHOTO/THINKSTOCK

Seafood and Chicken Gumbo

1 stick butter*
1 cup flour
1 small onion, diced
2 ribs celery, chopped
1 large bell pepper, chopped
2 garlic cloves, minced
3 quarts water
2 cups cubed chicken
1½ pounds fresh okra
1 can diced tomatoes
1 pound andouille sausage, sliced thin
1 teaspoon Fiesta Brand® Cayenne Pepper
1 teaspoon Fiesta Brand® Black Pepper
2 teaspoons salt
3 cups cooked small shrimp

In a hot skillet, melt butter and stir in flour. Cook over medium heat, stirring frequently until you have a dark brown roux. Add onion, celery, bell pepper and garlic; sauté until vegetables are tender, about 15 minutes. In a large stockpot, combine roux with water and remaining ingredients, except shrimp, and cook over medium-high heat, covered, about 30 minutes. Add shrimp and cook an additional 5 to 10 minutes. Serve hot with rice.

*For a healthier alternative, you can use Texas Pecan Oil instead of butter.

Texas Lobster Stew

4 cups cubed cooked lobster meat
¼ cup minced onion
Butter*
6 cups milk
2 cups heavy cream
Salt and Fiesta Brand® Black Pepper
1 teaspoon Fiesta Brand® Paprika
1 teaspoon Fiesta Brand® Chili Powder
Dash dry sherry
Cornmeal

I tried this dish at a seafood restaurant on the Texas Gulf Coast. It was so good, I decided to make my own version. It's a cross between a stew, soup and chowder.

In a large skillet, quickly brown lobster and onions in butter. Add milk; stir. Add remaining ingredients; simmer in hot skillet 15 to 20 minutes. Stir in a bit of cornmeal to thicken, if needed.

*For a healthier alternative, you can use Texas Pecan Oil instead of butter.

Texas Gulf Grouper Chowder

½ cup chopped onion
1 cup chopped carrots
1 rib celery, thinly sliced
2 tablespoons butter, divided*
2 medium potatoes, peeled and diced
1 Fiesta Brand® Whole Bay Leaf

1 teaspoon salt
¼ teaspoon each thyme and Fiesta Brand® Black Pepper
1 cup dry white wine or water
2 cups milk
1 grouper fillet, bite-size pieces

Combine all ingredients, except fish, in a saucepan. Cook over medium-high heat until potatoes are done. Stir in fish and continue to cook until fish is done.

*For a healthier alternative, you can use Texas Pecan Oil instead of butter.

Sweet Corn Chowder

½ pound bacon, cooked and
    crumbled
2 cups peeled and diced potatoes
1 onion, diced
1 cup water

2 cans cream-style corn
2 cups milk
Salt and Fiesta Brand® Black Pepper
    to taste
1 tablespoon butter*

Combine ingredients in a large saucepan and cook until potatoes are tender. Serve hot with cornbread on the side.

*For a healthier alternative, you can use Texas Pecan Oil instead of butter.

Sausage Frijole Chowder

1½ pounds ground sausage
2 cans pinto beans
1 can stewed tomatoes
2 cups milk
1 cup water
1½ cups diced potatoes
1 large onion, chopped

1 Fiesta Brand® Whole Bay Leaf
1½ teaspoons seasoned salt
1 teaspoon Fiesta Brand® Black Pepper
½ teaspoon minced garlic
½ teaspoon thyme
1 can green chiles

Brown sausage; drain. Combine with remaining ingredients and cook, covered, until potatoes are tender. Remove bay leaf. Stir with a fork to break up potatoes and beans; mix well. Serve hot.

Vegetable Chowder

4 carrots, diced
1 zucchini, diced
1½ cups broccoli
1 onion, chopped
1 cup chopped celery
1 can whole-kernel corn
1 can cream-style corn
½ cup all-purpose flour
½ teaspoon Fiesta Brand® Black Pepper
¼ teaspoon sugar
2 cups milk
1 can chicken broth
1 cup shredded Cheddar cheese
1 tablespoon minced jalapeño peppers

Combine all ingredients in a large saucepan and cook on low, covered, until veggies are tender. Stir occasionally and add milk to thin, if needed. Serve hot with a dash of fresh parsley and real bacon bits on top, if desired.

Chili

Chunky Texas Red Chili, page 67

Three Pepper & Bean Chili

2 pounds beef stew meat
2 green bell peppers, chopped
2 yellow bell peppers, chopped
2 jalapeño peppers, chopped
1 can black beans
1 can pinto beans
1 can chili beans
1 medium onion, chopped
2 stalks celery, chopped
4 garlic cloves, minced
2 tablespoons Fiesta Brand® Chili Powder
2 tablespoons cumin
1½ tablespoons Fiesta Brand® Cajun-All
1 Fiesta Brand® Whole Bay Leaf
2 cups water
2 cans tomatoes
1 can tomato paste
Salt and Fiesta Brand® Black Pepper

Brown meat and combine with all ingredients in a large pot. Cover and simmer until thickened. Serve hot with a slice of cornbread on the side.

Chunky Texas Red Chili

3 pounds beef stew meat
3 tablespoons olive oil*
2 tablespoons butter or margarine*
1 large green bell pepper, chopped
1 large onion, chopped
1 can tomato sauce
4 tablespoons Fiesta Brand® Chili Powder
1 tablespoon cumin powder
2 tablespoons minced fresh garlic
1 tablespoon chopped jalapeño pepper
1 tablespoon salt
1 tablespoon Fiesta Brand® Black Pepper
6 cups water
½ cup all-purpose flour

Cut stew meat into small pieces about ¼-inch in size; brown in a skillet with olive oil and butter. Combine browned beef and remaining ingredients in a large pot, and cook over medium heat about 2 hours. Add water as necessary to thin or additional flour to thicken.

*For a healthier alternative, you can use Texas Pecan Oil instead of olive oil and butter.

Texas Red Chili

2 pounds lean ground beef
1 pound ground sausage
6 cups water
¼ cup whiskey
2 tablespoons vegetable oil*
4 garlic cloves, peeled and chopped
2 teaspoons salt
7 tablespoons Fiesta Brand® Chili Powder

1 tablespoon ground cumin
1 tablespoon vinegar
2 teaspoons Fiesta Brand® Black Pepper
½ tablespoon Fiesta Brand® Crushed Red Pepper
2 tablespoons cornmeal
½ tablespoon hot sauce
1 tablespoon sugar

Brown ground beef and sausage together in a large skillet or pot. Drain fat and transfer to a large pot. Add remaining ingredients and stir to mix. Simmer over medium-low heat at least 2 hours. Stir often to break-up meat. Add more water or more cornmeal, for desired consistency.

*For a healthier alternative, you can use Texas Pecan Oil.

GEORGE EAGER, BOERNE

D.DZINNIK/ZOONAR/THINKSTOCK/

Texas Red-Hot Burning Chili

1½ pounds lean ground beef
1 pound hot country sausage
1 small onion, minced
6 cups water
2 tablespoons vegetable oil*
4 garlic cloves, minced
2 teaspoons salt
2 teaspoons Fiesta Brand® Black Pepper
2 tablespoons Fiesta Brand® Crushed Red Pepper
2 tablespoons red hot sauce
2 tablespoons minced jalapeño pepper
7 tablespoons Fiesta Brand® Chili Powder
1 tablespoon ground cumin
1 tablespoon apple cider vinegar
1 teaspoon horseradish
4 tablespoons cornmeal

Not for the faint of heart! This chili packs a punch with all kinds of ways to make your mouth steam.

Brown ground beef and sausage with onion; drain fat. Place meat into a large pot with water and remaining ingredients, except cornmeal. Cover and simmer 3 to 4 hours, adding water or beer as needed. About 30 minutes before serving, stir in cornmeal. Chili is done when it is thick enough to hold a spoonful of sour cream on top when serving in a bowl.

*For a healthier alternative, you can use Texas Pecan Oil.

Lip-Burning Meat-Lovers Chili

1 pound ground beef
½ pound ground sausage
½ pound ground goat
2 cups cubed cooked chicken
2 onions, chopped
1 can stewed tomatoes
3 tablespoons Fiesta Brand® Chili Powder
2 garlic cloves, minced
½ tablespoon Fiesta Brand® Oregano
½ tablespoon cumin powder
2 teaspoons Fiesta Brand® Crushed Red Pepper
2 jalapeño peppers, minced
2 cans green chiles
3 tablespoons hot sauce
4 cups water
3 chicken or beef bouillon cubes
3 tablespoons cornmeal

This chili is perfect for those who love meat... and heat! Of course you can calm this chili down a bit, but why mess with a good thing.

This is almost too easy. Cook all of the meat and drain. Combine all ingredients in a large pot and simmer until thickened. Add a beer to thin or some more cornmeal to thicken if needed. Serve hot.

Drunk Red Onion Chili

2 pounds ground beef or stew meat
2 large red onions
1 can diced tomatoes
1 can beer
2 shots tequila
Juice of 1 lime
2 beef bouillon cubes
1 can black beans
1 red bell pepper, diced

4 garlic cloves, minced
2 teaspoons salt
2 teaspoons Fiesta Brand® Oregano
1 tablespoon Fiesta Brand®
   Chili Powder
1 teaspoon each coriander and cumin
1½ teaspoons Fiesta Brand®
   Crushed Red Pepper
3 tablespoons flour

Brown beef and drain. In a large pot, combine all ingredients and simmer covered until thick. Serve hot.

Work Week Simple Border Chili

2 pounds lean beef, chopped
Oil*
1 pack chili seasoning mix
1 can frijoles, mashed
1 cup salsa
1 can beef stock
1 cup water (or more)

For those times when you need chili the quick and easy way, this recipe uses canned items and ingredients that are easy to find.

Brown stew meat in some oil. Combine with remaining ingredients in a large pot and cook over medium heat until thick. Serve hot.

*For a healthier alternative, you can use Texas Pecan Oil.

Herb's Chili

2 pounds hamburger meat (chuck)
2 pounds ground pork
2 cans pinto beans
2 cans chopped tomatoes
2 cans Ro-Tel (tomatoes with green chiles)
2 cans whole-kernel corn
2 packages Williams Chili Mix
1 jar pimentos
Jalapeños to taste (optional)
1 bell pepper, chopped
1 large onion, finely chopped
Salt and Fiesta Brand® Black Pepper to taste

Brown meat in large pot, add remaining ingredients plus enough water to desired thickness. Simmer at least 1 hour or as long as you can wait.

PUMP JACK CHILI COOK-OFF

Lone Star Chili

2 pounds hamburger, browned and drained
1 pound smoked sausage, browned and sliced
1 Lone Star beer
1 large onion, chopped
2 cans diced tomatoes
4 cans diced green chiles
2 cups water
2 teaspoons minced garlic
2 tablespoons Fiesta Brand® Chili Powder
Salt, Fiesta Brand® Black Pepper and hot sauce to taste

Combine all ingredients in a large pot and simmer until you're ready to eat.

Ground Beef Mole Chili

2 pounds ground beef, browned and drained
3 cups beef broth
5 squares chocolate
1 onion, chopped
1 red bell pepper, chopped
1 jalapeño pepper, chopped
4 tablespoons Fiesta Brand® Chili Powder
1 teaspoon each Fiesta Brand® Cinnamon and cumin powder
1 teaspoon each salt, Fiesta Brand® Black Pepper and
   Fiesta Brand® Crushed Red Pepper
1 can tomato soup
½ cup brewed coffee
1 tablespoon Fiesta Brand® Paprika

Boil beef broth in a large pot and stir in chocolate. Add in browned ground beef and remaining ingredients. Simmer 1 hour over medium-high heat and serve hot.

Jalapeno Chili

1 pound ground beef

5 jalapeño peppers, seeded and chopped

1 green bell pepper, chopped

1 onion, chopped

3 tablespoons Fiesta Brand® Chili Powder

1 cup salsa

1 tablespoon cumin powder

1 teaspoon Fiesta Brand® Onion Powder

1 teaspoon Fiesta Brand® Garlic Powder

1 dash lime juice

2 tablespoons sour cream

4 cups water

Brown ground beef and drain. Combine all ingredients in a pot and cook for an hour over medium-high heat.

PRAIRIE DOG CHILI COOK-OFF AND WORLD CHAMPIONSHIP OF PICKLED QUAIL EGG EATING

April • Grand Prairie

Dozens of chili cooks compete in several divisions during this Texas-size salute to the official state dish. Held at Traders Village, other contests include Head to Head Banana Racing, the always popular Lemon Roll and Team Tortilla Toss Contest. The World Championship of Pickled Quail Egg Eating Contest is always a crowd pleaser. Contestants compete to see who can consume more of these hard-boiled gourmet delights within the 60-second time limit. This event brings together families, friends, and fun.

972.647.2331 • www.tradersvillage.com

Refried Bean Chili with Corn & Onion Topping

Chili:

2 pounds hamburger, browned and drained
2 cups water
1 large onion, chopped (reserve 2 tablespoons for topping)
2 cans diced tomatoes with juice
2 cans refried beans
2 cans green chiles with juice
½ tablespoon minced garlic
2 tablespoons Fiesta Brand® Chili Powder
2 teaspoons salt
2 teaspoons Fiesta Brand® Black Pepper
2 teaspoons cumin powder

Topping:

2 tablespoons chopped onion
1 small can whole-kernel corn, drained
Hot sauce to taste
Fiesta Brand® Cilantro to taste
Tortilla chips

Combine chili ingredients in pot and simmer 1 to 2 hours adding water to thin or cornmeal to thicken, if desired. While chili is cooking, combine chopped onion and corn with hot sauce and cilantro to taste; chill. Serve chili in a bowl with a few chips on top to create a platform then spoon topping over top. Serve immediately.

Goat & Tomato Chili

Goat meat is a traditional choice for many Texas chili recipes.

2 pounds goat meat
1 cup chopped onion, divided
1 can tomato paste
3 cans tomato sauce
1 large can stewed tomatoes
1 green bell pepper

2 jalapeño peppers
2 tablespoons Fiesta Brand® Chili Powder
1 tablespoon Fiesta Brand® Paprika
½ tablespoon cumin powder
1 Fiesta Brand® Whole Bay Leaf
1 can kidney beans, optional

Brown goat meat in a skillet with ½ cup chopped onion and drain off any grease. In a large pot, combine meat with remaining ingredients and cook over low heat several hours. If desired, add beans last and continue to cook just until heated through.

Green Pork Chili

1 (3-pound) pork roast
2 cans diced tomatoes, drained
2 cans green chiles
4 diced jalapeños
2 green bell peppers, finely chopped
1 large onion, finely chopped
1 tablespoon minced garlic
Salt and Fiesta Brand® Black Pepper to taste
1 tablespoon Fiesta Brand® Chili Powder
1 tablespoon chopped parsley

Grill or cook pork in an oven until done; remove excess gristle and chop or shred. In a large stockpot, combine all ingredients and water to cover. Cook on low, covered, at least 4 hours.

Dutch Oven Cooking

Lone Star Pepper Bread

2½ cups self-rising flour
½ cup all-purpose flour
¼ cup brown sugar
1 teaspoon baking powder
½ teaspoon each salt and Fiesta Brand® Onion Powder
1 teaspoon each Fiesta Brand® Garlic Powder and Fiesta Brand® Crushed Red Pepper
1 can Lone Star beer
¼ cup butter or margarine, melted*

Using your hands, mix all ingredients, except butter, in a large bowl. Form into a nice dough and place in a well-greased, cast-iron Dutch oven. Pour melted butter over dough and cover with lid. Cook with coals on bottom and coals on top. Bread is done when toothpick inserted into middle comes out clean. Usually around 45 minutes.

*For a healthier alternative, you can use Texas Pecan Oil instead of butter.

Dutch Oven Shrimp Chowder

2 tablespoons butter*
1 medium onion, chopped
3 cans potato soup
3½ cups milk

2 tablespoons Old Bay seasoning
1 can cream-style corn
2 pounds medium shrimp, peeled
1½ cups shredded Monterey Jack cheese

Melt butter in Dutch oven; add onion and sauté until tender. Stir in soup, milk and seasoning; bring to a boil. Add corn and shrimp; continue to cook, stirring often, for approximately 5 minutes or until shrimp is pink. Stir in cheese until melted. We use a 12-inch Dutch oven with 8 coals on the lid and 16 under the oven.

*For a healthier alternative, you can use Texas Pecan Oil instead of butter.

LESLIE & JOHNATHAN SCHAFFT, KAST IRON KOOKERS, GREENVILLE

Senator Tommy Williams Beef Stew

1 or 2 pounds stew meat
Salt and Fiesta Brand® Black Pepper to taste
Hot water to cover
2 bouillon cubes
1 medium onion, chopped
1 can diced tomatoes
1 tablespoon parsley flakes
Dash Worcestershire sauce
5 or 6 carrots, sliced
8 or 9 potatoes, peeled and cubed

Texas Senator Tommy Williams was one of several legislators who saw the importance of preserving the cooking heritage of the great state of Texas. Because of their efforts, the cast-iron Dutch oven was named the official cooking implement for the Lone Star State. It was won in 2005 with Senate Concurrent Resolution No. 9, 79th Legislature, Regular Session.

Trim meat, season with salt and pepper, and brown over fire. Add HOT water to more than cover meat. Add bouillon, onions, tomatoes, parsley and Worcestershire, cover and cook about 1 hour. Add carrots and potatoes; continue cooking—the longer the better.

TEXAS STATE SENATOR TOMMY WILLIAMS AND HIS WIFE MARSHA

Texas State Capitol
Austin

Tex-Mex Corn Chili

2 tablespoons vegetable oil*
2 pounds beef steak, cubed
3 garlic cloves, minced
1½ teaspoons flour
4 tablespoons Fiesta Brand® Chili Powder
2 cups water
1 can whole-kernel corn
Salt to taste

Heat oil in Dutch oven. Brown meat working in batches. Return all meat to pot and stir in garlic; cook 10 minutes. Sprinkle with flour; cook 1 minute longer. Add chili powder, water, corn and salt. Cover and cook at a simmer for 45 minutes.

*For a healthier alternative, you can use Texas Pecan Oil.

HOLLAND CORN FESTIVAL

Holland • June

For more than 34 years, Holland has celebrated their "local cash crop" with the Holland Corn Festival. Events include a parade, 5K run, contests, street dance, barbecue cook-off, arts, crafts, carnival and much more.

254.760.3204 • www.hollandcornfest.org

SANDRA CUNNINGHAM/HEMERA/THINKSTOCK

Leslie's Dutch Oven Taco Soup

1 pound ground chuck
1 onion, chopped
2 teaspoons minced garlic
1 can whole-kernel corn
1 can cream-style corn
1 large can diced tomatoes
2 cans tomato sauce
1 can chili hot beans with juice
1 can hot Ro-Tel tomatoes
1 can black beans
1 can red kidney beans
1 package dry taco seasoning
1 package dry Hidden Valley Ranch dressing
1 small can chopped jalapeños

Brown beef with onion and garlic. Add remaining ingredients and water to desired consistency. Cook 30 to 45 minutes. Delicious served over corn chips and topped with sour cream, cheese and extra jalapeños. You will need a 14-inch or larger Dutch oven—this makes a lot of soup—with 10 coals on top and 18 under. We usually line the Dutch oven with aluminum foil to keep the tomato sauce from damaging seasoned oven, and it makes clean-up easier.

LESLIE & JOHNATHAN SCHAFFT
KAST IRON KOOKERS IDOS BRANCH, GREENVILLE

Carne Asada

3 pounds cheap steak
¼ cup each lime juice, lemon juice and orange juice
½ cup water
1 tablespoon minced garlic
1 onion, finely chopped
1 teaspoon Fiesta Brand® Black Pepper
1 teaspoon hot sauce
1 tablespoon chili sauce
½ tablespoon Fiesta Brand® Ground Italian Spice Blend (Italian seasoning)

Slice steak into small pieces and pound to tenderize, if needed. Combine all ingredients in a zip-close bag and marinate a few hours (the longer the better). Pour into a Dutch oven and cook 1 hour over hot coals.

Texas-Style Pecan Chicken

1 chicken, cut-up
2 cans cream of chicken soup
1 tablespoon Fiesta Brand® Chili Powder
1 onion, diced

1 cup chopped pecans
5 to 6 potatoes, diced
6 carrots, diced

Place chicken in bottom of a Dutch oven. Combine soup, chili powder and onion; pour over chicken. Sprinkle with about ⅓ of the pecans. Layer on potatoes and sprinkle with pecans. Add carrots and sprinkle with remaining pecans. Cook in a traditional cast-iron Dutch oven for about 1 hour. You can also cook in the oven or even a crockpot.

Chile Relleno Casserole

1 pound bulk pork sausage
1 small onion, chopped
2 eggs, beaten
2 cups salsa
2 cans green chiles
1 cup milk
1 tablespoon flour

1 cup shredded Monterey Jack
cheese
1 tablespoon Fiesta Brand® Chili
Powder
½ tablespoon thyme
1 teaspoon sugar

Brown pork with onion; drain fat. Combine with remaining ingredients in a large bowl and mix well. Pour into a Dutch oven, cover and cook over coals until thick.

The horns of Texas longhorn cattle can extend up to 120 inches tip to tip.

MIKE FLIPPO/HEMERA/THINKSTOCK

Frijoles and Sausage

1 pound ground sausage, browned
3 cans pinto beans
1 onion, diced
1 green bell pepper, diced
Salt and Fiesta Brand® Black Pepper to taste
Dash each cumin powder and Fiesta Brand® Chili Powder
½ tablespoon each vinegar and hot sauce

Drain grease from browned sausage. Combine everything in a Dutch oven and stir to mix. Cook over coals 30 to 45 minutes or until thickened and bubbly. Serve hot.

Potatoes Dutch-Oven Style

12 strips bacon, chopped
1 small onion, chopped
½ cup chopped green bell pepper
½ tablespoon minced garlic
5 baking potatoes, cubed

1 small can chopped mushrooms
1 can cream of mushroom soup
1 cup shredded pepper jack cheese

In a Dutch oven over hot coals, cook bacon, onion and green pepper until bacon is done. Add garlic and potatoes; cook another 15 minutes, stirring often. Stir in mushrooms and soup; cook 25 minutes longer, stirring frequently. Remove from heat and cover with cheese. Serve when cheese is melted.

Hash-Brown Potato Casserole

1 (32-ounce) package frozen shredded
   potatoes
1 can cream of chicken soup
1 (12-ounce) package shredded Cheddar
   cheese
1 (8-ounce) carton sour cream
1 teaspoon salt
1 small onion, finely chopped
1 cup melted butter, divided*
2 cups crushed cornflakes

Place thawed potatoes on bottom of 12-inch Dutch oven. Combine soup, cheese, sour cream, salt, onion and ½ cup melted butter; pour over potatoes. Top with crushed cornflakes and drizzle remaining melted butter over all. Put 10 coals on top of oven and 14 coals on bottom. Cook 45 to 55 minutes.

*For a healthier alternative, you can use Texas Pecan Oil instead of butter.

LESLIE & JOHNATHAN SCHAFFT
KAST IRON KOOKERS IDOS BRANCH, GREENVILLE

Pumpjacks, like this one south of Midland, are a common sight in West Texas.

GINAE MCDONALD/ISTOCKPHOTO/THINKSTOCK

Black Forest Cobbler

2 tablespoons butter*
1 (18-ounce) box devil's food cake mix
1 (12-ounce) can Sprite
1 can cherry pie filling

Spread butter on bottom of Dutch oven. Sprinkle cake mix evenly over butter. Add ½ can Sprite; stir. Spoon pie filling over top (do not stir). Cover with lid. Put 8 to 10 charcoal briquettes on bottom, 16 to 18 on top. Cook 35 to 40 minutes.

*For a healthier alternative, you can use Texas Pecan Oil instead of butter.

SEYMOUR CHAMBER OF COMMERCE

We use these Dutch oven cobbler recipes at our chili cook-offs. Each year at our May Fish Day event, we have a cook-off division called "the surprise box" category. All the ingredients needed to make the cobbler are placed in a box. Each contestant picks a box, which they take back to their camp to cook and be judged. Each contestant has a different box and a different recipe. They are always excited to see what they get to cook each year.

FISH DAY

May 1st • Seymour

Across the country, numerous fishing events happen throughout the year but none are like Seymour's unique Fish Day which began in 1926. In those days, the first day of fishing season was May 1st. After Lake Kemp was built, everyone went fishing on that day leading Seymour's forefathers to make it a holiday since everyone skipped school, left the farm, and closed the shops to go fishing. The Seymour Chamber of Commerce added a little fun to the day by adding additional events like a chili cook-off, three-legged race, horseshoe tournament and more.

940.889.2921 • seymourtxchamber.org

Dutch Oven Swirl Cobbler

2 tablespoons butter*
2 (16-ounce) cans crushed pineapple

1 (18-ounce) box yellow cake mix
1 (12-ounce) can Sprite

Spread butter on bottom of Dutch oven. Drain fruit; pour over butter. Sprinkle cake mix evenly over top. With your finger, make a swirl in the mix. Pour in Sprite. Cover with lid. Put 8 to 10 charcoal briquettes on bottom, 16 to 18 on top. Cook 50 minutes to 1 hour.

*For a healthier alternative, you can use Texas Pecan Oil instead of butter.

SEYMOUR CHAMBER OF COMMERCE

Weapons have been chosen for the cow patty toss. Let the games begin!
Fish Day, Seymour

Charlie's Peach Pastel

1 stick butter*
1 cup sugar
1 cup flour
1 cup milk
1 (12- to 16-ounce) can peaches
1 teaspoon Fiesta Brand® Cinnamon
1 teaspoon allspice
1 teaspoon baking powder

Melt butter in a 14-inch Dutch oven. Combine all other ingredients and pour into Dutch oven. Cook until crust is browned to your liking.

*For a healthier alternative, you can use Texas Pecan Oil instead of butter.

CHARLIE TOMLIN, SOUTH TEXAS

PEACH FESTIVAL

Second Saturday in July • Parker County

Parker County is known as the Peach Capital of Texas. The Peach Festival began 24 years ago as a small festival and has grown to an average attendance of 30,000. You can find handmade arts and crafts and any type of food or beverage that can include peaches. Peach Pedal is for the bike-riding enthusiast.

1.888.594.3801
www.weatherford-chamber.com

Vegetables & Other Side Dishes

Karen's Chuck Wagon Beans

½ pound bacon
3 pounds ground beef
3 cups chopped onions
1 cup chopped celery
2 beef bouillon cubes
⅔ cup water
1½ garlic cloves, crushed
1½ cups ketchup
3 tablespoons mustard
1½ teaspoons salt
½ teaspoon Fiesta Brand® Black Pepper
2 (29-ounce) cans molasses-style baked beans
Dash liquid smoke

Karen says, "We have had these beans at EVERY family reunion or gathering, probably for the past 40 years. My Mom would fill a large crockpot and all my brothers would dig in, much to the dismay of their wives!! And now it's a favorite with my son's baseball team."

Heat oven to 375°. Fry bacon until crisp; set aside. Drain fat from pan. Add beef, onion and celery; cook until brown. Boil water in microwave or on stovetop; dissolve bouillon cubes in boiling water. Add all ingredients, except reserved bacon, into meat mixture. Cover and bake 1 hour until hot and bubbly. Crumble bacon over top and serve.

KAREN CAMPBELL, WOODLANDS

How to make Frijoles

2 cups dried pinto beans
¼ pound salt pork
1 large onion, chopped
1 garlic clove, minced

1 tablespoon Fiesta Brand® Chili Powder
¼ teaspoon ground cumin
¼ teaspoon Fiesta Brand® Garlic Powder
½ teaspoon Fiesta Brand® Oregano

Soak pinto beans in water overnight. Next day, poke salt pork with a knife or fork several times. Pour soaking water off beans and place in a large pot. Add fresh water to cover by at least an inch. Add salt pork, onion, garlic, chili powder, cumin, garlic and oregano. Simmer on low heat at least 4 hours or until water is absorbed and mixture is thick. For whole bean frijoles, do not over-stir or beat for a semi-mashed version. Serve hot.

Texas Trail Rider Pinto Beans

2½ pounds pinto beans
1 pound ham hocks
2 onions, chopped
4 tablespoons sugar
2 cans green chiles

1 can tomato paste
Dash Fiesta Brand® Cayenne Pepper
Salt and Fiesta Brand® Black Pepper
   to taste

Clean beans and soak overnight. Next day, combine beans with remaining ingredients and water to cover. Cook over low heat until beans are tender stirring occasionally. Add water, if needed, while cooking.

Big Red's Texas-Style Pinto Beans

2 pounds dry pinto beans
2 cured hamhocks (or 6 slices bacon)
1 tablespoon granulated onion
1 tablespoon Fiesta Brand® Chili Powder
1 teaspoon granulated garlic
¼ teaspoon Fiesta Brand® Black Pepper
½ teaspoon ground cumin
1 teaspoon chicken bouillon
1 teaspoon light brown sugar
1 teaspoon salt

Wash beans and pour into a 5-quart pot with 6 cups water; bring to a boil and cook 3 minutes. Cover and remove from heat; let rest 30 minutes. Return to heat, bring to a boil, and cook 1 hour. Add ham and remaining ingredients. Cook, covered, 2 hours or until done. Adjust salt to your taste.

DORIS COATS, FORMER CASI TERLINGUA CHILI
CHAMPION (AND ONE FINE BEAN COOK),
INTERNATIONAL BAR-B-QUE COOKERS ASSOC. COOK-OFF

INTERNATIONAL BAR-B-QUE COOKERS ASSOCIATION COOK-OFF

October • Grand Prairie

One of the largest BBQ events in Texas, more than 100 cookers prepare as many as 600 judging samples in a number of competitions including the Obie-Cue Backyard BBQ Championship, International Bar-B-Que Cookers Association Invitational, Jackpot Beans and a kid's cook-off. Barbeque cooks and cooking devices are a show in themselves when serious beef barons showcase custom-made, unique traveling pits with individual touches of creativity. While the competition can become serious, the atmosphere and camaraderie is strictly fun-filled recreation.

972.647.2331 • www.tradersvillage.com

Texas-Style Hot Mixed Beans

2 cans pork and beans
1 can kidney beans
1 can black beans
1 can pinto beans
3 jalapeño peppers, diced
½ tablespoon Fiesta Brand® Cayenne
   Pepper

2 tablespoons brown sugar
1 teaspoon Fiesta Brand® Black Pepper
1 tablespoon Fiesta Brand® Chili Powder
½ pound salt pork, cubed (1x1x¼-inch)
1 large onion, chopped
2 garlic cloves, minced

Combine everything in a large pot. Cook very slowly 1 hour or longer.

Southwestern Sizzler Beans ala Charra

1 (1-pound) bag dried beans
1 cup finely chopped white onion
5 teaspoons chopped fresh garlic
2 tablespoons TSS Southwestern Sizzler
   seasoning
1 teaspoon sea salt

2 slices bacon
⅓ bunch cilantro, finely chopped (plus more
   for garnish, if desired)
2 to 3 large fresh Roma tomatoes, peeled
   and chopped

Rinse beans, cover in water and soak 2 hours. Drain, rinse again and cover beans with water by 3 inches. Bring to a boil and cook about 20 minutes. Reduce heat to medium, adding water if needed (do not drown in water though). Add onion and garlic; continue to cook 45 minutes. Reduce heat to low. Add additional water, if needed, seasonings, bacon, cilantro and tomatoes. Cook 1 hour longer or until beans are soft and soup is thick. Garnish with fresh cilantro, if desired.

TEXAS SELECT SEASONINGS

Grillin in Groves Baked Beans

4 strips bacon
1 medium onion, chopped
1 small bell pepper, chopped
2 cans pork & beans
1 can jalapeño ranch-style beans
2 tablespoons Worcestershire sauce
2 tablespoons mustard
½ cup ketchup
½ cup BBQ sauce

This recipe is a favorite with the cook teams!

Sauté bacon, onion, and bell pepper in a skillet until soft. Combine with remaining ingredients in an oven-safe dish. Bake at 350° for 30 minutes.

ANDREA SKJOLD/ISTOCK/THINKSTOCK

Lone Star Beer Baked Beans

1 pound small white beans
4 cups water
1 onion, chopped
3 tablespoons maple syrup
1 tablespoon brown sugar
¼ cup ketchup

3 tablespoons yellow mustard
1 teaspoon salt
1 teaspoon Fiesta Brand® Black Pepper
1 teaspoon hot sauce
1 cup chopped bacon (not cooked)
2 or 3 bottles Lone Star beer

In a large pot, bring beans and water to a boil; boil 2 minutes and turn off heat. Let stand for 1 hour then drain off water. Place beans in a large oven-safe baking dish. Add onions, syrup, brown sugar, ketchup, yellow mustard, salt, black pepper and hot sauce; mix well. Place bacon over beans pushing some into beans. Pour two beers slowly over top. Add a third beer, if needed. Bake, covered, at 325° for 2 hours or more until beans are tender. Remove cover and bake until top is browned and bacon is done. Serve hot.

Refried Beans & Onions

2 cans pinto beans
1 tablespoon salt
1 tablespoon minced garlic
1 tablespoon sugar

¼ cup bacon drippings
½ teaspoon hot sauce
Minced onion
Fiesta Brand® Paprika

Combine all ingredients, except onion and paprika; cook over medium heat while mashing with a potato masher. Do not over-mash, leave a few large pieces for texture. Add salt, if needed, to taste. Serve hot topped with minced onion and paprika.

Refried Black Beans

2 cans black beans, drained and
   rinsed
1 cup water
3 tablespoons vegetable oil*
1 large onion, diced
1½ teaspoons salt

1 tablespoon cumin
½ cup shredded white American
   cheese
Green onions and green peppers,
   chopped (optional)

Purée 2 cans black beans with 1 cup water in a food processor. In a saucepan, sauté onions in oil; stir in salt and cumin powder. Add beans, mix well and continue to cook until heated through. Serve hot topped with white cheese and chopped green onions and peppers, if desired.

*For a healthier alternative, you can use Texas Pecan Oil.

Austin cityscape as viewed from the Colorado River.

HARRIS SHIFFMAN/ISTOCKPHOTO/THINKSTOCK

Southwestern Sizzler Spanish Rice

1 cup long grain rice (not instant)
¼ cup oil
Salt
2 to 3 cloves fresh garlic, chopped
½ cup minced white onion

1 (10-ounce) can chopped tomatoes
   with green chilies, undrained
1¾ cups water, divided
2 tablespoons TSS Southwestern Sizzler
   seasoning

Brown rice in oil until light golden brown. Season to taste with salt. Add garlic and onion; sauté about 3 minutes. Add tomatoes with green chilies, 1½ cups water and TSS Southwestern Sizzler seasoning. Bring to a boil. Cover, reduce heat and simmer 15 minutes or until rice becomes moist and excess water is cooked down.

TEXAS SELECT SEASONINGS

Seasoned Salsa Rice with Black Beans

1½ cups water
1 cup instant brown rice
1 can black beans, drained and rinsed
1 cup salsa

1 teaspoon Fiesta Brand® Cajun-All
1 teaspoon cumin powder
Cilantro leaves and parsley (optional)

Bring water to a boil in a medium saucepan. Add remaining ingredients. Reduce heat to low, cover and simmer 10 minutes. Fluff with fork before serving. Top with cilantro leaves or parsley before serving, if desired.

Texas-Style Green Bean Casserole

3 cans green beans, drained
1 can green chiles, drained
Salt and Fiesta Brand® Black Pepper
2 cups ham, cubed
½ stick butter, melted*

1 tablespoon hot sauce (optional)
1 cup sour cream
½ cup crushed tortilla chips
½ cup Mexican melting cheese (or white American)

Place all ingredients, except cheese, in a treated baking dish. Bake at 350° for 30 minutes. Top with cheese and bake until melted and golden. Serve hot.

*For a healthier alternative, you can use Texas Pecan Oil instead of butter.

Field Peas with Snaps

2 cups water
1 beef bouillon cube
2 cups frozen field peas with snaps

1½ teaspoons salt
Dash olive or canola oil*

Bring water with beef bouillon cube to a boil. Add peas and return to boil; turn down to simmer and cover with lid. Simmer about 30 minutes then add salt. Simmer another 10 minutes then add oil. To thicken, remove lid and mash a few peas against side of cooker. Peas should be tender with somewhat thick juice. Serve warm.

*For a healthier alternative, you can use Texas Pecan Oil.

FROM THE RECIPE COLLECTION OF BELLE GOODMAN
SUBMITTED BY PAULETTE GOODMAN, JEFFERSON

Tangy Green Beans

2 cans green beans
2 tablespoons red wine vinegar
2 tablespoons olive oil*
2 tablespoons Dijon mustard
Salt and Fiesta Brand® Black Pepper to taste
½ cup sliced onion
2 tablespoons grated Parmesan cheese

Combine all ingredients, except cheese, in a saucepan. Boil until reduced, place in serving dish and sprinkle with Parmesan cheese. Serve hot.

*For a healthier alternative, you can use Texas Pecan Oil instead of olive oil.

EDITH64/ISTOCK/THINKSTOCK

Peas and Carrots... and Chiles

1 tablespoon oil*
2 cups thinly sliced carrots
½ cup sliced seeded jalapeño peppers
2 tablespoons water
½ teaspoon tarragon
¼ teaspoon salt
⅛ teaspoon Fiesta Brand® Black Pepper
1½ cups fresh snow peas, cut in thirds

In large skillet, heat oil over high heat. Stir in carrots, peppers, water, and seasonings. Cook covered about 5 minutes. Stir in snow peas and cook an additional 5 minutes. Serve hot.

*For a healthier alternative, you can use Texas Pecan Oil.

Carrot Souffle

3 pounds carrots, cooked in boiling
   water
1½ cups butter*
6 large eggs

¼ teaspoon Fiesta Brand® Cinnamon
1 tablespoon baking powder
3 cups sugar
½ cup all-purpose flour

Process carrots until well mashed. Combine with remaining ingredients and process until smooth. Pour in lightly greased pan and bake 1 hour or until set.

*For a healthier alternative, you can use Texas Pecan Oil instead of butter.

CAJUN FRENCH & MUSIC FEST, ANHALT

Cotija Cheese and Corn

2 cans whole-kernel corn
1 cup shredded cotija cheese
4 tablespoons mayonnaise
3 tablespoons sour cream
½ tablespoon Fiesta Brand® Chili Powder
½ tablespoon Fiesta Brand® Black Pepper
½ tablespoon cumin powder
1 teaspoon Fiesta Brand® Cilantro

Cotija (known as Queso Anejado or "aged cheese") is aged and sold in small rounds or large blocks. Salty and pungent, the moist version is a bit like Feta. The more common version is very firm, more like Parmesan. Cotija is excellent crumbled and used in tacos, soups, salads or over beans.

In a skillet or saucepan bring corn to a boil. Boil off excess water. Remove from heat and add in remaining ingredients. Serve warm.

Bacon-Wrapped Corn on the Cob

1 to 2 ears of corn (with husks) per person
1 bacon strip per ear of corn (or butter*)
Fiesta Brand® Chili Powder
Fiesta Brand® Black Pepper

Gently pull husks away from corn, but do not remove. Remove silk and sprinkle corn with chili powder and pepper to taste. Wrap corn with a slice of bacon (may baste with butter rather than using bacon). Put husks back in place and tie with baking string or a bit of foil. Grill until husks are dry and begin to darken. Remove from heat, carefully open. Remove bacon, if desired (if bacon is crispy enough, some like to eat it as well). Serve hot.

*For a healthier alternative, you can use Texas Pecan Oil instead of butter.

Fiesta Fried Corn

4 slices bacon, cooked and crumbled
2 cans whole-kernel corn
1 red bell pepper, chopped
1 can green chiles, drained
1 teaspoon sugar
½ cup milk
2 tablespoons butter*
Salt and Fiesta Brand® Black Pepper,
   to taste

In a large skillet, fry bacon until crisp. Remove, crumble, and return to skillet with drippings. Stir in corn, bell pepper, chiles, sugar and milk. Return to heat and cook over medium-high heat. Stir in butter, salt and pepper. Stir until liquid has cooked away.

*For a healthier alternative, you can use Texas Pecan Oil instead of butter.

Baked Hominy and Squash

1 pound yellow squash
2 tablespoons corn oil*
½ medium onion, chopped
1 red bell pepper, diced
1 jalapeño, chopped
¼ teaspoon Fiesta Brand® Oregano
¼ cup milk
1 can hominy
2 tablespoons sour cream
1 cup shredded Cheddar cheese
1 cup crushed tortilla chips

Wash and chop squash; set aside. In a skillet over medium heat, combine oil and onion, cook until golden. Stir in squash, bell pepper, jalapeño and oregano; continue cooking until vegetables are tender. Stir in milk, hominy and sour cream. Remove from heat and spoon into a prepared baking dish. Top with cheese and crushed tortilla chips. Bake at 350° about 20 to 25 minutes. Serve hot.

*For a healthier alternative, you can use Texas Pecan Oil.

Asadero and Cheddar Noodles

1 (9-ounce) package macaroni noodles
½ cup shredded Asadero cheese
½ cup shredded Cheddar cheese
¼ teaspoon salt
¼ cup milk
Dash Fiesta Brand® Black Pepper
Fiesta Brand® Crushed Red Pepper

Cook pasta in boiling unsalted water until done. Drain and rinse with fresh hot water. In a saucepan, cook remaining ingredients over low heat until cheese is melted. Add pasta and toss until well coated. Serve hot

MSHELDRAKE/ISTOCK/THINKSTOCK

Cast-Iron Skillet Okra

1 pound okra
1 cup cornmeal
½ cup very finely crushed tortilla chips
Salt and Fiesta Brand® Black Pepper

Pinch Fiesta Brand® Cayenne Pepper
Pinch Fiesta Brand® Garlic Powder
Milk
Oil or butter*

Wash okra, removing stems and bad spots. Slice into bite-sized pieces. Combine cornmeal, tortilla chips, salt, pepper, cayenne pepper and garlic powder. Dip okra in a bit of milk and dredge in cornmeal mixture, turning until coated evenly. Heat some oil or butter in a cast-iron skillet. Cook over medium heat turning until all sides are golden. Drain on a paper towel for a minute and serve hot.

*For a healthier alternative, you can use Texas Pecan Oil.

Slightly Mashed Taters

8 or 9 red potatoes
⅓ cup milk
3 tablespoons butter*
2 teaspoons Fiesta Brand® Garlic Powder

1 cup cooked and crumbled bacon
Salt and Fiesta Brand® Black Pepper to
  taste

Clean potatoes and peel, if desired. Place in a pot with ⅓ cup milk, water to cover and butter. Boil until potatoes are soft; drain. Place potatoes in a baking dish and break up gently with a fork (do not cream or mash). Stir in bacon, sprinkle with salt and pepper. Broil for a few minutes to brown top. Serve hot.

*For a healthier alternative, you can use Texas Pecan Oil instead of butter.

Fried Cabbage

4 slices bacon
1 medium head cabbage, coarsely chopped
1 medium onion, diced
1 can mild Ro-Tel tomatoes
1 (14½-ounce) can diced tomatoes
1 teaspoon minced garlic
Water, about ½ of diced tomato can
Salt and Fiesta Brand® Black Pepper to taste

Fry bacon in a large skillet; remove to drain and set aside. Gradually add cabbage and onions to hot bacon grease stirring frequently. When browned, add remaining ingredients. Simmer, covered, until cabbage is tender (25 to 35 minutes) stirring several times. Crumble bacon and add to cabbage just before serving.

Variations: Adding frozen or canned whole-kernel corn adds color. Fried Cabbage is good with smoked sausage, but I think cooking them together diminishes the flavor of both. Instead, cut slits on both sides of sausage and brown well in broiler, pour off grease, slice and serve on top of Fried Cabbage.

SANDRA K. FITE, GILMER

Not long after my husband Paul and I were married, and after I had served him steamed cabbage for about the third time, he said "Why don't you fix fried cabbage like my mother does?" That went over real big! I envisioned rolling cabbage leaves in batter and frying them in oil. The original recipe is actually just cabbage stir-fried with some water added and cooked, covered, until tender. Over the years, my Fried Cabbage has evolved to this variation.

Cast-Iron Skillet Asparagus with Texas Pecans

½ cup chopped pecans
1½ tablespoons olive oil*, divided
1 pound fresh asparagus, halved
¼ cup water

1 teaspoon sugar
¼ teaspoon salt
¼ teaspoon Fiesta Brand® Black Pepper
1 teaspoon lemon juice

In a cast-iron skillet over medium-high heat, brown chopped pecans in ½ tablespoon olive oil until lightly browned. Place on a paper towel. In same skillet, sauté asparagus in 1 tablespoon olive oil. When edges are browned, add water, sugar, salt and pepper and cook until water boils off. Serve hot sprinkled with lemon juice and browned pecans.

*For a healthier alternative, you can use Texas Pecan Oil instead of olive oil.

The Lighthouse formation in Palo Duro Canyon State Park. Canyon (near Amarillo)

MIKE NORTON/ISTOCKPHOTO/THINKSTOCK

Easy Broccoli & Cheese Frittata

3 large eggs
1½ cups milk
2 cups broccoli pieces
1 can green chiles, drained
1 teaspoon cumin powder
Salt and Fiesta Brand® Black Pepper
Dash hot sauce
Dash Fiesta Brand® Garlic Powder
1 tablespoon olive oil*
½ cup mild shredded Cheddar cheese

Traditionally, this dish is cooked half-way through in a small hot skillet then broiled to a golden finish and served open-face (unlike its folded cousin, the omelet). This baked version makes a perfect side dish.

Combine all ingredients in an oven-safe dish; stir well. Bake at 400° for 10 to 15 minutes or until eggs are set and top is golden.

*For a healthier alternative, you can use Texas Pecan Oil instead of olive oil.

Sweet Onion Pie Supreme

1 baked pie shell
4 cups thinly sliced sweet onions
3 tablespoons butter or margarine*
1½ cups sour cream
2 tablespoons flour
½ cup milk
1 teaspoon salt
2 eggs, well beaten
2 to 3 slices bacon, cooked crisp and crumbled
⅓ cup shredded Cheddar cheese
2 green onions, chopped

Preheat oven to 325°. Cook onion in butter until lightly golden brown, spoon into pie shell. Combine sour cream with flour; add milk, salt, and beaten eggs. Pour over onions bake 30 minutes, or until center is firm. Garnish with bacon, cheese and green onions.

*For a healthier alternative, you can use Texas Pecan Oil instead of butter.

TEXAS RIO GRANDE VALLEY ONION FESTIVAL

TEXAS RIO GRANDE VALLEY ONION FESTIVAL

First Saturday in April • Weslaco

Onion Fest celebrates the development of the world-famous Texas 1015 Onion developed in Weslaco by Dr. Leonard Pike. Sweet onion blossoms, dancing horse shows, onion eating contests, recipe contests, and a wide mix of musical entertainment come together for this sweet celebration held the first Saturday in April in Weslaco, Texas.

956.968.2102 • www.weslaco.com

Baked Onion

6 medium onions
Olive oil*
2 cups chicken broth
Fiesta Brand® Chili Powder, salt and Fiesta Brand® Black Pepper to taste
Hot sauce and Worcestershire sauce to taste
Shredded cheese

Cut off ends of each onion. Peel only the thin, paper-like outer layer. Place in a baking pan, brush with olive oil, and let rest 5 minutes to allow oil to seep in between the layers. Pour chicken broth over onions, cover and let rest at room temperature about 30 minutes. Bake at 375° for 1 hour or until soft. Carefully peel back outer skin with a fork and fold back some of the layers to make gaps. Sprinkle with seasonings, hot sauce and Worcestershire to taste; cover with cheese. Return to oven until cheese is melted. Serve hot.

*For a healthier alternative, you can use Texas Pecan Oil instead of olive oil.

Riverwalk
San Antonio

Executive Trail Ride Vegetable Mix

1 medium yellow squash, sliced
1 medium zucchini squash, sliced
2 medium onions, sliced
1 cup sliced mushrooms
3 carrots, chopped
1 green bell pepper, sliced
1 red bell pepper, sliced
2 whole mild chiles, chopped
2 tablespoons olive oil*
½ teaspoon salt
½ teaspoon Fiesta Brand® Black Pepper
2 garlic cloves, crushed
Dash Fiesta Brand® Cilantro
Dash cumin powder
Dash thyme
2 tablespoons fresh and finely chopped oregano and/or basil

Combine everything and toss to evenly coat. Separate into portions and wrap in foil. Cook on the grill over hot coals (or bake in oven at 350°) until vegetables are tender. Serve hot.

*For a healthier alternative, you can use Texas Pecan Oil instead of olive oil.

Beef

Mama's Roast with Brown Gravy, page 128

Big Texan Steak Ranch is a Living Legend

When people hear the word "Texan," they automatically think "Big." When you pair the biggest and the best food and a true western experience, you get the world's most famous restaurant. The Big Texan Steak Ranch in Amarillo, Texas, is a living legend.

Ranch is an important word in Texas, sparking images of tender beef, hands dedicated to the Brand, and a warm "Howdy." That's what founder R.J. "Bob" Lee created when coming to Texas more than half a century ago.

Lee grew up on the lore of the Old West. When he arrived, he went looking for a good steak, served with Texas flair. Failing to find one, he turned his disappointment into determination and his dreams into reality.

The Big Texan Steak Ranch opened on Old Route 66 in 1960. Lee understood the lure of the Old West and used billboards to let travelers know about his restaurant. A mounted horseman waved to travelers and gave them another reason to stop. A lanky metal cowboy that loomed above the unique architecture of the first building still welcomes travelers to The Big Texan.

The story of the FREE, 72-ounce steak is legendary. Cowboys from working ranches were regulars at the Big Texan. Good natured bragging turned into a contest one night, and the winner consumed 4½ pounds of steak, a baked potato, salad, shrimp cocktail and dinner roll before he finished. The original meal and rules are still in place: Complete it in one hour; don't leave the table until you're finished; and, if you lose your dinner you lose the contest.

Today, the Big Texan Steak Ranch sprawls alongside Interstate 40, featuring a motel with a Texas-shaped swimming pool, horse hotel, gift shop, candy store and micro-brewery.

7701 Interstate East 40 • Amarillo, Texas 79118-6915
(806) 372-1000 • www.bigtexas.com

Baby Back Ribs with Coffee Bourbon BBQ Sauce

2 racks baby back ribs
1 cup bourbon whiskey
¼ cup vegetable oil*
1 cup chopped yellow onion
1 tablespoon Cajun Spice Mix (recipe follows)
1 teaspoon Fiesta Brand® Crushed Red Pepper
2 teaspoons minced garlic
1 jalapeño pepper, seeded and minced
1 teaspoon grated lemon zest

1 cup ketchup
¾ cup brewed strong black coffee
½ cup brown sugar
¼ cup each red wine vinegar and fresh lemon juice
2 tablespoons each Worcestershire sauce and dark molasses
1 tablespoon hot red pepper sauce

Rinse ribs and set aside allowing to dry completely. In a small saucepan, over medium-high heat, simmer bourbon until reduced to ⅓ cup. Remove from heat and cool. Heat oil in a large saucepan over medium-high heat. Add onion, Cajun spice and red pepper flakes; cook 3 minutes. Add garlic, jalapeño and lemon zest; cook 30 seconds stirring constantly. Add remaining ingredients; heat to simmer. Add cooled bourbon and cook 2 minutes, stirring. Purée in food processor, in batches, until smooth. Cover ribs (2 whole racks) with sauce and marinate 12 to 24 hours in refrigerator. Cook over medium heat 10 to 15 minutes each side.

Cajun Spice Mix:

2½ tablespoons Fiesta Brand® Paprika
2 tablespoons each salt and Fiesta Brand® Garlic Powder
1 tablespoon each Fiesta Brand® Black Pepper, Fiesta Brand® Onion Powder, Fiesta Brand® Cayenne Pepper, Fiesta Brand® Oregano and thyme

Mix well, store in covered container or zip-lock bag.

*For a healthier alternative, you can use Texas Pecan Oil.

RECIPE PROVIDED BY HOUSTON LIVESTOCK SHOW AND RODEO™
WORLD'S CHAMPIONSHIP BAR-B-QUE COMMITTEE

Dr. Pepper Grilled Beef Ribs

4 to 5 pounds beef ribs
3 cans Dr. Pepper (not diet)
2 tablespoons hot sauce
1 large onion, chopped
3 tablespoons brown sugar

4 tablespoons vinegar
2 to 4 tablespoons Worcestershire sauce
¼ cup ketchup
1 cup barbecue sauce

Combine all ingredients in a stockpot and cook, covered, on low about 2 hours. Remove ribs and grill over medium-high heat until done basting with cooking sauce. (If finishing in an oven, place ribs in an oven-safe dish and coat with sauce. Bake at 325° until rib meat pulls away from bone. Cover lightly with foil and baste as needed.) Serve hot.

Dr. Pepper was invented in Waco, Texas, at Morrison's Old Corner Drug Store. It is the oldest of the major brand soft drinks in America. Charles Alderton, a young pharmacist working at Morrison's store, is credited as being the inventor of the famous drink. Alderton spent most of his time mixing up medicine for the people of Waco, but in his spare time he liked to serve carbonated drinks at the soda fountain. He kept a journal of his recipes, and after numerous experiments he finally hit upon a mixture of fruit syrups that he liked.

Grilled Texas-Style Beef Brisket

6 to 8 pound boneless beef brisket
1¼ cup finely chopped onion, divided
2 teaspoons Fiesta Brand® Paprika
½ teaspoon freshly ground Fiesta Brand® Black Pepper
2 cups steak sauce, divided
2 tablespoons butter*
1 cup ketchup
1 tablespoon brown sugar
¼ teaspoon Fiesta Brand® Crushed Red Pepper

Preheat grill with very low coals. (Single layer of coals with space between each.) Trim fat from brisket to ¼-inch. Combine ¾ cup onion, paprika and black pepper. Rub evenly over surface of brisket. Place brisket, fat side up, in large disposable pan; add ½ cup water. Cover pan tightly with aluminum foil. Place in grill, close cover, and cook 5 hours, turning brisket over every 1½ hours. As brisket cooks, remove fat with a baster as it accumulates in pan, add additional ½ cup water as needed, and/or add briquets as needed to keep coals at a very low temperature. After 5 hours cook time, remove foil from pan. Remove brisket and place on grid directly over very low coals. Reserve 1 cup pan drippings. Mix remaining pan drippings with 1 cup steak sauce; brush over brisket. Close grill cover and continue cooking 1 hour, brushing occasionally with sauce. Meanwhile, cook remaining ½ cup finely chopped onion in butter until tender. Stir in remaining 1 cup steak sauce, reserved pan drippings, ketchup, brown sugar and crushed red pepper. Simmer 10 minutes. Serve with the brisket.

*For a healthier alternative, you can use Texas Pecan Oil instead of butter.

THE TEXAS BEEF COUNCIL

Oven-Baked Texas BBQ Beef Brisket

1 whole brisket
½ cup Fiesta Brand® Chili Powder
½ cup salt
¼ cup granulated garlic
¼ cup granulated onion
¼ cup Fiesta Brand® Black Pepper
¼ cup sugar
2 tablespoons dry mustard
2 Fiesta Brand® Whole Bay Leaves
1 can beef broth

Combine dry ingredients; mix well. Season brisket on both sides with dry ingredients and place in roasting pan. Roast in a preheated 350° oven for 1 hour. Combine beef broth with equal amount of water. Add enough liquid to roasting pan to achieve ½-inch liquid in pan. Cover roasting pan, lower heat to 325°, and continue cooking 4 to 5 hours, basting frequently. Remove from oven when instant read thermometer registers 185°. Let rest 15 minutes before slicing. Trim all fat and slice meat thinly across the grain.

THE TEXAS BEEF COUNCIL

TAYLOR INTERNATIONAL BARBEQUE COOK-OFF

August • Taylor

In addition to the Barbecue Cook-off, this fun event features an arts and crafts show. The Taylor International Barbeque Cook-off always proves to be an enjoyable home-town type festival where people watch the antics of the teams just being themselves. All proceeds go to local charities so come out, bring your appetite for some of the best barbeque, relax, and enjoy yourself.

512.352.6364 • www.taylorjaycees.org

ITSTOCK FREE/ POLKA DOT/THINKSTOCK

Brisket the Easy Way

1 market-trimmed brisket
Yellow mustard
Texjoy steak seasoning (or your favorite dry seasoning mix)
¼ cup pickled jalapeño peppers

Jane says, "This recipe is easy and spicy... just the way us Texans like it."

Wash and dry brisket. Place on heavy-duty foil. Rub brisket with yellow mustard. Generously season with Texjoy Steak Seasoning. Sprinkle jalapeños and some juice from peppers around brisket. Wrap tightly in foil. Bake at 400° 1½ hours. Reduce temperature to 250° and bake 5 hours or until done to your liking.

JANE CARTER, VIDOR

George's "Jorge's" Grilled Rib-Eye Steak

2 (or more) rib-eye steaks
Salt
Fiesta Brand® Black Pepper
Fiesta Brand® Garlic Powder
Fiesta Brand® Cilantro
(Or Hog Wild brand seasoning)

"Rub it, beat it with a fork, leave it alone for a while, grill it, then eat. That's about it!" George says.

Wash steaks; dry on paper towels. Combine rub ingredients using equal parts of each; amounts will vary depending on how many steaks you have and how big they are. Poke steaks with a fork a few times and work rub mix into meat. Place on a plate and let rest until grill is ready. Cook over medium-high heat with plenty of smoke. Turn once. Allow to rest a few minutes before serving.

GEORGE EAGER, BOERNE (GATEWAY TO THE HILL COUNTRY)

Minced Jalapeno Cast-Iron Seared Steak with Tequila Cream Sauce

Steaks:

2 to 4 steaks, your choice of cut
Butter*
1 can green chiles
1 tablespoon minced jalapeño pepper
½ small onion, minced
1 tablespoon lemon juice
Salt and Fiesta Brand® Black Pepper to taste
Dash steak sauce

Tequila Cream Sauce:

1 cup sour cream
1 tablespoon tequila or flavored rum
1 teaspoon brown sugar
1 teaspoon Fiesta Brand® Chili Powder
1 teaspoon cumin powder
Fiesta Brand® Cilantro to taste

In a cast-iron skillet over medium-high heat, sear outside of steaks in butter. Add remaining steak ingredients and coat steaks while they cook. You can fully cook steaks on stove or finish them in the oven using the cast-iron skillet as a baking dish. While steaks are cooking, combine cream sauce ingredients and chill before serving. This sauce breaks down quickly so do not keep leftovers. Serve steaks hot with Tequila Cream Sauce drizzled over and/or served on the side.

*For a healthier alternative, you can use Texas Pecan Oil instead of butter.

Rusty's Salt 'n Pepper Steaks with Bean Salsa

Bean Salsa:

1 (15-ounce) can black beans, drained
3 tomatoes, seeded and chopped
1 jalapeño pepper, seeded and diced
½ small sweet onion, chopped
¼ cup chopped fresh cilantro
½ teaspoon grated lime rind
3 tablespoons fresh lime juice
½ teaspoon salt
½ teaspoon Fiesta Brand® Black Pepper

Roughly chop beans in food processor; do not puree them. Stir in remaining ingredients. Serve over Fiesta Steak. Makes 3 cups (extra salsa can be refrigerator).

Salt 'n Pepper Steaks:

4 rib-eyes or filets
½ cup Dale's marinade (or your favorite marinade)
Salt
Fresh Cracked Pepper

Marinate steaks in Dale's for a few minutes. Remove and rub with salt and pepper. (Don't just sprinkle; rub salt and pepper into meat.) Grill over high heat or skillet-cook to your liking. Before serving, allow steaks to rest a few minutes and sprinkle lightly with more cracked black pepper. Serve topped with Bean Salsa.

RUSTY EAGER, BOERNE (GATEWAY TO THE HILL COUNTRY)

Lone Star Beer Grilled Porterhouse

2 to 4 porterhouse steaks
1 Lone Star beer
1 can chopped mushrooms
Salt and Fiesta Brand® Black Pepper
Fiesta Brand® Chili Powder
Fiesta Brand® Garlic Powder

Place steaks in a glass baking dish and cover with Lone Star beer. Use enough to drench steaks. Cover with mushrooms, salt and pepper to taste, and a dash each of chili powder and garlic powder. Cover and chill 30 minutes. Flip steaks; season again with salt and pepper to taste and a dash each of chili powder and garlic powder. Marinate another 30 minutes. Remove steaks from marinade and grill. Serve hot.

This simple recipe uses only a few ingredients including a Texas icon—Lone Star Beer!

TEXAS REDS STEAK & GRAPE FESTIVAL
June • Bryan

Texas Reds Steak & Grape Festival is a celebration of the beef and wine industries and their impact on our community. We're talking about a Steak Cook-off, Texas Wine tasting, grilling exhibitions, live entertainment, children's activities and much more—all smack dab in Historic Downtown Bryan, where the slogan "The Good Life Texas Style" was born.

979.209.5528 • www.texasredsfestival.com

Fiesta Rib-Eye Steaks

4 beef rib-eye or top loin steaks, cut ¾-inch thick
2 tablespoons fresh lime juice, divided
8 (6-inch) flour tortillas
¼ cup shredded Colby cheese
¼ cup shredded Monterey Jack cheese
1 cup salsa

Place beef steaks in a glass dish. Sprinkle with 1 tablespoon lime juice, turn and sprinkle with remaining lime juice. Place steaks over medium coals. Grill 7 to 9 minutes for rare (140°F) to medium (160°F), turning once. While steak is cooking, wrap tortillas securely in heavy duty aluminum foil. Place tortilla packet on outer edge of grill and heat 5 minutes, turning once. Top each steak with an equal amount of cheese 1 minute before removing from grill. Serve with salsa and tortillas.

THE TEXAS BEEF COUNCIL

Speedy Beef Kabob Tacos

2 pounds beef stew meat
1 envelope taco seasoning
1 cup chopped onion
Taco shells
Salsa
Lettuce
Shredded cheese

In a skillet, brown stew meat and break into small pieces; drain. Add taco seasoning and water as called for per package directions. Stir in onions and cook until onions are tender. Serve in taco shells with heated salsa, lettuce, cheese and/or other favorite toppings.

Chicken Fried Steak with White Gravy

Steak:

8 tenderized beef cutlets, at room temperature
3 eggs
2 cups milk
1 tablespoon Worcestershire sauce
3 cups flour
½ cup finely crushed tortilla chips
2 teaspoons Fiesta Brand® Seasoning Salt
2 cups oil*

Gravy:

Grease from cooking steaks
1½ cups flour
Garlic salt
Fiesta Brand® Black Pepper
1 (8-ounce) can evaporated milk
1 cup water

Whisk eggs, milk and Worcestershire sauce. Combine flour, crushed tortillas and meat seasoning in another bowl. Dip each cutlet in egg mixture then dredge in flour mixture. Dip again in egg wash, and very gently place in a skillet with hot oil. Cook until breading is set and golden brown. Carefully remove steaks from skillet and drain on a platter lined with paper towels. In same skillet, reduce heat and very carefully stir in gravy ingredients. Cook, stirring constantly, until well mixed, even and hot. Serve Chicken Fried Steaks covered with White Gravy.

*For a healthier alternative, you can use Texas Pecan Oil.

Margarita Beef with Orange Salsa

Margarita Beef:

1½ pounds well-trimmed top-round steak, cut 1-inch thick
⅔ cup frozen orange juice concentrate, thawed
½ cup tequila
⅓ cup fresh lime juice
2 tablespoons olive oil*
2 tablespoons chopped fresh ginger
2 medium garlic cloves, crushed
1 teaspoon each salt and Fiesta Brand® Oregano
¼ teaspoon Fiesta Brand® Crushed Red Pepper
Cilantro sprigs and lime wedges for garnish

Place steak in plastic bag. Combine remaining ingredients, except garnish; add to bag, turning to coat. Close bag securely and marinate in refrigerator 4 hours to overnight. Remove steak from marinade; discard marinade. Place steak on grill over medium coals. Grill 22 to 26 minutes for medium rare (150°) to medium (160°) doneness, turning once. Remove steak to carving board; let stand 10 minutes. Carve steak crosswise into thin slices; arrange on serving platter. Garnish with cilantro and lime. Serve with Orange Salsa.

Orange Salsa:

2 oranges, peeled and cut into ½-inch pieces
1 small red or white onion, chopped
1 jalapeño pepper, seeded and finely chopped
¼ cup chopped fresh cilantro
2 to 3 tablespoons fresh lime juice
2 tablespoons olive oil*
½ teaspoon salt
½ teaspoon Fiesta Brand® Oregano

Combine all ingredients in non-metallic bowl and refrigerate at least 1 hour.

*For a healthier alternative, you can use Texas Pecan Oil instead of olive oil.

THE TEXAS BEEF COUNCIL

Shredded Beef Stuffed Peppers

1 pound beef roast or shredded beef steak
Olive oil*
1 cup rice
1 can tomato soup
1 tablespoon minced garlic
1 can whole-kernel corn
1 cup salsa
½ tablespoon Fiesta Brand® Cilantro
1 teaspoon cumin powder
1 teaspoon Fiesta Brand® Chili Powder
Lemon juice, salt and Fiesta Brand® Black Pepper to taste
4 to 6 green, yellow or red bell peppers, halved

Brown meat in a hot skillet with a small amount of olive oil. Do not over-cook; leave lots of pink. Combine with remaining ingredients, except bell peppers; stuff bell peppers. Cook at 350° until pepper begins to soften and brown around edges. Serve hot. For an added bonus, include cheese, jalapeño or even refried beans.

*For a healthier alternative, you can use Texas Pecan Oil instead of olive oil.

Easy Salsa Black Bean Beef Fajitas

2 tablespoons oil*
2 large shank steaks, cut into strips
Dash each cumin powder, Fiesta Brand® Chili
    Powder, lemon or lime juice
1 onion, cut into strips
2 bell peppers, cut into strips
Salt and Fiesta Brand® Black Pepper

1 can black beans, drained
1 cup medium salsa
Flour tortillas
2 tablespoons butter, softened*
1½ cups grated cheese
1 pint sour cream

Stir fry steak in large skillet with oil, cumin, chili powder, lemon or lime juice, onions, and peppers. Season with salt and pepper; stir in black beans and salsa. Continue to cook, stirring constantly, until everything is hot and mixed well. Remove from heat. Spoon onto lightly butter tortillas with a slotted spoon. Top with cheese and sour cream. Serve hot.

*For a healthier alternative, you can use Texas Pecan Oil.

John Bremond House
Austin

TIMSDD/ ISTOCKPHOTO /THINKSTOCK

Chili Cheese Empanadas

2 cups flour
1 teaspoon salt
2 teaspoons baking powder
2 tablespoons solid vegetable shortening

Milk
1 can chili without beans
1 cup shredded cheese
2 cups vegetable oil*

Sift flour, salt and baking powder. Cut in shortening until mixed. Add enough milk to moisten dough. (If dough becomes sticky, add a bit more flour.) On a lightly floured surface, roll dough to ¼-inch thick. Cut into circles using a large cookie cutter, cup or large-mouth jar mouth. Re-form extra dough and repeat until dough has been completely used. Mix chili and cheese; place equal portions in middle of each circle. Fold dough over in half and pinch edges together. Fry empanadas in hot oil until golden brown, turning once. Serve hot after draining on paper towels.

*For a healthier alternative, you can use Texas Pecan Oil.

Empanada comes from the Spanish word empanar for "to bake a pastry." These Mexican and Spanish specialties are usually single-serving turnovers with a pastry crust and savory meat-and-vegetable filling. They can also be filled with fruit and served as dessert. Empanadas range in size from the huge empanada gallega, large enough to feed a large family, to empanaditas, tiny ravioli-size pastries.

Texas-Style Beef Pot Roast

3 to 4 pound beef roast
1 (1-pound) bag baby carrots
2 cups chopped onion
10 red potatoes, quartered

1 cup water
1 envelope onion soup mix
1 packet taco seasoning

Combine roast, veggies and water in large roasting pan. Sprinkle half the seasoning packets over roast and sprinkle rest into water. Cover with fitted lid or foil. Bake at 325°, basting as needed, until roast pulls with fork.

RUSTY EAGER, BOERNE (GATEWAY TO THE HILL COUNTRY)

Sunday Beef Roast

1 (3- to 4-pound) roast
1 (1-pound) bag baby carrots, thickly sliced
2 onions, chopped in large pieces
10 red potatoes, quartered
4 banana peppers, chopped
1 envelope dry onion soup mix
½ cup leftover coffee
Salt and Fiesta Brand® Black Pepper to taste
1 cup water

Place roast and veggies in a large oven-safe dish. Add remaining ingredients. Bake at 350°, covered, basting as needed, approximately 2 hours or until roast is tender and can be pulled with a fork. Add water as needed. Uncover last 15 minutes to brown edges.

Mama's Roast with Brown Gravy

1 (3- to 4-pound) roast
1½ teaspoons salt
1 teaspoon Fiesta Brand® Black Pepper
1½ teaspoons rubbed sage
4 small onion slices
2 cups water
⅓ to ½ cup flour
Kitchen Bouquet, optional

Rub salt, pepper and sage on both sides of roast. Place 2 small slices of onion under roast in a covered roasting pan and 2 slices onion on top of roast. Pour 2 cups water in pan (do not pour over roast). Put lid on roaster and cook 2½ to 3 hours in 325° oven. Remove from roaster and place on platter. To make gravy, mix ⅓ to ½ cup flour in enough water to make a paste. Add to juices from roast, stirring until thick. For a browner more flavorful gravy, add a few drops of Kitchen Bouquet.

CAROLYN ADAMS, ELECTRA

This roast is a favorite dish my mother often serves on Fridays, when her four daughters and their children and grandchildren come home for lunch. Having lunch at my Mom's on Friday has been a ritual for at least twenty-five years. Her great-grandson Nick calls her the Gravy Granny, because he loves her roast gravy so much.

Pauline (Barker) Mieir was born and grew up on a farm in Wilbarger County Texas, near the Red River. She attended Harrold, Texas schools, and is a retired nurse. Pauline is the mother of five children, ten grandchildren, six great grandchildren, and one great-great grandchild. She is a member of the Faith Baptist Church in Iowa Park, Texas.

Black-Eyed Pea Jambalaya

1 pound ground beef
1 cup cubed ham
1 medium onion, chopped
½ cup chopped bell pepper
2 cups rice
1 can black-eyed peas, drained (reserve juice)
1 teaspoon salt
1 teaspoon Fiesta Brand® Black Pepper
½ cup green onions, tops only
1 teaspoon parsley
Hot sauce, optional

Brown ground beef in a large skillet. Add ham, onion and pepper; cook until vegetables are soft. Add rice and continue to cook until it begins to fry. Add water to juice from black-eyed peas to make 2½ cups liquid; add to skillet. Cook, stirring frequently, about 40 minutes. Add salt and pepper just before removing from heat. Stir in black-eyed peas. Stir in green onions and parsley. Add hot sauce to taste, if you want it hot!

CAJUN FRENCH & MUSIC FEST, ANHALT

Classic Frito Pie

4 cups Fritos corn chips
1 small onion, chopped (divided)
1 cup grated Cheddar cheese (divided)
2 cups canned or homemade chili

Fritos were invented in Texas!

Spread 2 cups Fritos in a baking dish; sprinkle half the onion and half the cheese over the top. Pour chili over onion and cheese. Top with remaining 2 cups Fritos, onion and cheese. Bake at 350° 15 to 20 minutes or until cheese is bubbly. Serve hot.

Frito Meatloaf

1½ pounds ground beef
2 eggs
2 tablespoons milk
½ cup taco sauce
2 teaspoons Fiesta Brand® Black
   Pepper

2 teaspoons salt
1 cup crushed Fritos
1 small onion, minced
1 can green chiles
1 cup salsa

Combine all ingredients, except salsa, in a large bowl and form into meatloaf shape. Bake at 350° about 30 minutes. Cover with salsa and continue baking about 10 minutes or until meatloaf is done. Slice and serve hot.

Texas Bob's Mexican Meatloaf Foil Dinner

4 (18x12-inch) sheets heavy-duty aluminum foil
½ cup Pace picante sauce, divided
½ cup finely crushed tortilla chips
1 medium onion, chopped
1 package McCormick Original Taco Seasoning, divided
1 pound extra-lean ground beef
4 medium potatoes, peeled and cut length-ways
¼ cup chopped pickled jalapeños
1 cup shredded Cheddar cheese, optional

Bob McSpadden, or Texas Bob, loves the state of Texas and has a soft spot in his heart for Texas-style cooking, history and more. Bob and his wife love to travel the Lone Star state camping and seeing sights. Here is a Texas Bob camping favorite!

Preheat oven to 450°. Spray foil with nonstick cooking spray. Combine ¼ cup Pace picante sauce, tortilla chips, chopped onion, and ½ package taco seasoning; mix in ground beef. Shape into four meat loaves. Place each on a sheet of aluminum foil. Add potatoes, remaining taco seasoning and chopped jalapeños. Pour remaining ¼ cup Picante sauce over top. Bring up foil sides. Double fold top and ends to seal the packet; leave room for heat to circulate inside. Repeat to make four packets. Bake 30 to 35 minutes on a cookie sheet in oven. (These can also be grilled 18 to 22 minutes or cooked in a campfire full of good coals for 12 to 18 minutes.) Sprinkle cheese over top before serving.

BOB "TEXAS BOB" McSPADDEN

Meatloaf – No Ketchup

2 pounds lean ground beef
1 pound medium or hot pork sausage
2 eggs
1 bell pepper, diced
1 teaspoon celery seed (or ¾ cup diced celery)

3 tablespoons flour
1 teaspoon each thyme and salt
1 onion, diced
5 to 6 thick slices bacon

Mix everything except bacon and form into a loaf in a shallow pan lined with foil. Place bacon strips across top next to each other so that one strip will be with each slice. Bake at 375° about 1 hour and 15 minutes. When almost done, pour off excess grease.

SANDRA K. FITE, GILMER

Baked Cattleman's Pie

1 pound ground beef, cooked and drained
1 can tomato soup
1 can whole-kernel corn, drained
1 can green beans, drained
½ tablespoon Fiesta Brand® Chili Powder
2 uncooked deep-dish pie shells
2½ cups mashed potatoes
2 cups queso blanco, Chihauhua or other Mexican melting cheese

A delicious version of the traditional Shepherds Pie with a bit of a Tex-Mex twist!

Combine cooked beef, tomato soup, corn, beans and chili powder. Pour in 2 prepared pie shells. Gently cover each pie with equal amounts potatoes and bake at 300° for 1 hour. Top with cheese and bake until cheese is melted. For more flavor, add jalapeño or crushed red chiles. Serve hot.

Spanish Rice with Beef

1 pound ground beef
½ cup thinly sliced onion
1 can Pearl brand beer
⅓ cup diced green pepper
2 cups instant rice
1½ cups hot water
¼ cup bacon drippings or butter*
2 cans tomato sauce
1 teaspoon salt
1½ teaspoons Fiesta Brand®
   Chili Powder
Salt and Fiesta Brand® Black Pepper

Pearl Beer has been around since the 1800's in Texas but the original formula comes from Germany and was named "Perle." The name was changed to Pearl around 1886. A huge brewery in San Antonio, Texas, produced the beer for decades. Over the years the Pearl name has been bought and sold, but the beer is still being produced under contract in Fort Worth, Texas. The original Pearl Brewery in San Antonio is home to a large down town revitalization project is home to many shops and restaurants.

Brown ground beef with onion. Pour in beer and cook over medium heat until liquid is almost completely cooked off. Add in green pepper, instant rice, water and remaining ingredients; mix well. Bring to a boil, then reduce heat and simmer uncovered 5 minutes. Serve hot.

*For a healthier alternative, you can use Texas Pecan Oil instead of butter.

Everything's Bigger in Texas Burgers

Slaw:

¾ cup mayonnaise

2 tablespoons sugar

8 cups shredded green cabbage

¼ cup finely chopped onion

Salt and freshly ground Fiesta Brand® Black Pepper

Burgers:

2 pounds ground beef chuck

Vegetable oil, for rubbing*

Salt and freshly ground Fiesta Brand® Black Pepper

¾ cup barbecue sauce, divided

4 hamburger buns

Sliced pickles

Combine Slaw ingredients and set aside while preparing burgers. Heat grill. Form beef into 4 patties; rub with oil and season with salt and pepper. Sear over high heat, turning once, until cooked to preferred doneness. Brush with ½ cup barbecue sauce and continue to grill just until glazed, about 1 minute per side. Grill buns until toasted and brush with remaining barbecue sauce. Top burgers with pickles and slaw; serve.

*For a healthier alternative, you can use Texas Pecan Oil.

The Hamburger is a part of Athens, Texas heritage. A local man, Fletcher Davis (1864-1941) created and served the sandwich first at the Athens Brick yard and later at a lunch counter on the Athens Town Square from 1884 until the early 1900's. The sandwich was served with just-out-of-the-oven slices of homemade bread, garnished with ground mustard mixed in mayonnaise, a big slice of Bermuda onion and sliced cucumber pickles. Locals liked the sandwich so much that they raised funds to send him to the 1904 St. Louis World's Fair to introduce the sandwich.

Range Rider Roast Beef Sandwich

1 pound left-over roast beef, sliced or deli roast beef
1 envelope brown gravy mix
Water as called for in brown gravy mix
1 onion, sliced
1 bell pepper, sliced
Pepper jack cheese, if desired
4 to 8 slices Texas toast

This a great recipe for camping—it's quick and easy and you can spice it up some with your favorite seasoning.

Mix gravy per directions on package (you want a thick mixture). Coat roast beef with gravy. Make a sandwich combining meat coated with gravy, sliced onions, peppers and cheese. Wrap in foil and cook over embers of a fire or over medium heat. Turn as needed. Cook for a few minutes to allow cheese to melt. (Can also be baked in a 300° oven.) Serve hot.

Trail Ride Sloppy Joes

1½ pounds ground beef
½ pound shank steak
2 tablespoons vinegar
2 tablespoons mustard
2 tablespoons Worcestershire sauce
1 tablespoon hot sauce
½ cup ketchup
1 cup water
1 beef bouillon cube
2 cans tomato sauce
1 medium onion, chopped
1 can green chiles
1 garlic clove, minced
Salt and Fiesta Brand® Black Pepper to taste
6 to 8 slices Texas toast
6 to 8 pepper jack cheese slices

This Lone Star State version of Sloppy Joes includes beef, peppers and hot sauce served over Texas Toast and topped with pepper jack cheese.

Brown ground beef and shank steak. Shred or chop steak into small pieces. Combine all ingredients, except Texas toast and cheese, in a large pot and simmer until hot and excess water is reduced. Serve hot over Texas toast topped with pepper jack cheese.

Pork

Spicy-Apple-Glazed Pork Butt, page 147

Honey-Pecan Pork Cutlets

1 pound boneless pork cutlets, ¼-inch-thick
½ cup all-purpose flour
3 tablespoons butter, divided*
¼ cup honey
¼ cup chopped pecans

Ken Horton of the Texas Pork Producers Association says this award-winning recipe is a favorite around the office. "Debra Tanner of Port Lavaca, Texas was a First Place Winner with her 'Honey-Pecan Pork Cutlets.' It is simple to make, has a great flavor and includes a favorite product from Texas and the south, pecans."

Dredge cutlets in flour, shaking off excess. Heat 1 tablespoons butter in heavy skillet over medium heat. Add cutlets and brown on both sides, about 5 to 6 minutes. Stir together remaining butter, honey and pecans; add to skillet, stirring gently. Cover and simmer gently 7 to 8 minutes. Remove cutlets to serving platter; pour sauce over.

*For a healthier alternative, you can use Texas Pecan Oil instead of butter.

COURTESY OF DEBRA TANNER, PORT LAVACA
SUBMITTED BY THE TEXAS PORK PRODUCERS ASSOCIATION

Pan-Seared Pork Chops

Olive oil*
2 to 4 pork chops
Salt and Fiesta Brand® Black Pepper
¼ cup minced onion

1 tablespoon minced garlic
3 tablespoons apricot preserves
Sliced almonds

In a skillet, sear pork chops in olive oil. Do not fully cook. Sprinkle with salt and pepper, minced onion and garlic; continue to cook until done. Reduce heat. Add apricot preserves to glaze chops. Tope with sliced almonds. Serve hot.

*For a healthier alternative, you can use Texas Pecan Oil instead of olive oil.

C. L. JOHNSON, HOUSTON

Pork Tenderloin with Herb Sauce

1 pork tenderloin
1 tablespoon melted butter*
3 tablespoons minced onion
1 tablespoon minced garlic
1 green chili pepper, minced
½ cup chicken broth

2 tablespoons Dijon or spicy brown
  mustard
½ tablespoon rosemary
½ tablespoon thyme
½ tablespoon Fiesta Brand® Black Pepper
1 teaspoon salt

Place tenderloin in a glass baking dish. Combine remaining ingredients and pour over tenderloin. Coat evenly and cover. Chill overnight if possible. Grill over medium heat, pan cook, or bake at 300° until done. When done, slice into thin slices and serve hot over pintos or rice.

*For a healthier alternative, you can use Texas Pecan Oil instead of butter.

Houston

ANTHONY TOTAH/HEMERA/THINKSTOCK

Chicken-Fried Jalapeno Pork Chops

4 to 6 bone-in pork chops
Salt and Fiesta Brand® Black Pepper
⅔ cup flour
1 cup finely crushed tortilla chips
½ teaspoon Fiesta Brand® Chili Powder
½ teaspoon Fiesta Brand® Paprika
Dash Fiesta Brand® Garlic Powder

1 egg, slightly beaten
½ cup milk
1 jalapeño pepper, minced
2 teaspoons hot sauce
1 teaspoon steak sauce
Oil*

Sprinkle chops with salt and pepper on both sides. In a large bowl, combine flour, tortilla chips, chili powder, paprika and garlic powder. In another bowl, combine egg, milk, jalapeño pepper, hot sauce and steak sauce; mix well. Coat chops in egg mixture, then flour mixture; repeat if needed. Cook chops in a skillet with hot oil until golden brown. Remove to a paper towel for 1 to 2 minutes before serving. Serve hot.

*For a healthier alternative, you can use Texas Pecan Oil.

Texas-Style Pork Ribs

2 tablespoons finely ground Fiesta Brand®
  Black Pepper
1 tablespoon Fiesta Brand® Oregano
1 tablespoon Fiesta Brand® Paprika

½ tablespoon cumin powder
2 teaspoons celery salt
½ teaspoon Fiesta Brand® Cayenne Pepper
2 racks St. Louis-cut ribs

Combine dry ingredients and firmly rub into ribs. Cover and set aside. Ready grill or smoker to a temperature of around 300°. Place ribs in covered grill or smoker and cook, bone side down, about 15 minutes. Flip and cook another 15 minutes or until rack relaxes and droops when you lift it at the center. Cover tips with foil if burning starts. Serve hot.

Pepper Jelly Pork Ribs

2 racks pork ribs
1 tablespoon Fiesta Brand® Chili Powder
1 tablespoon cumin powder
1 tablespoon Fiesta Brand® Paprika

½ tablespoon garlic powder
½ tablespoon salt
1 teaspoon brown sugar
Pepper jelly

Remove membrane from back of ribs. Combine dry ingredients into a dry rub. Rub ribs down and grill, bake or smoke at 250° about 3 hours, covered and with lid closed. Remove ribs and coat with pepper jelly; wrap tightly in foil. Cook 1 hour longer or until ribs begin to fold or bend when picked up in the center. Ribs are done when bones twist from meat with little or no effort. Serve hot.

GBH007/ISTOCK/THINKSTOCK

Spicy Mustard-Glazed Pork Ribs

2 to 4 racks ribs
½ cup mustard
⅔ cup orange juice
⅓ cup pepper jelly
½ teaspoon ginger
Salt and Fiesta Brand® Black Pepper to taste
1 tablespoon soy sauce

These ribs pack some punch— lots of flavor with a tangy kick!

Remove membrane from back side of ribs. Combine remaining ingredients in a bowl and brush on pork ribs frequently while you grill or smoke over medium heat or bake at 300°. Serve hot when bones twist from meat with ease.

Cheesy Pork Quesadillas

1 pound pork chops, cubed small
Oil*
1 tablespoon lemon or lime juice
1 tablespoon each ground cumin and Fiesta Brand® Chili Powder
1 teaspoon Fiesta Brand® Cayenne Pepper
Salsa or diced onions and peppers
4 to 6 (6-inch) flour tortillas
8 to 12 slices white American deli cheese

In a skillet, brown pork in oil; add lemon or lime juice, cumin, chili powder, cayenne pepper and salsa. Continue to cook until heated through. Spray a tortilla with nonstick spray or spray butter on one side. Lay treated side down on hot nonstick skillet and quickly place a slice of cheese on one side. Top with meat filling and another slice of cheese. Fold tortilla over and cook until golden, flipping as needed. Serve hot topped with favorite taco toppings.

*For a healthier alternative, you can use Texas Pecan Oil.

Shredded Tex-Mex Pork

5 pounds pork shoulder roast
Oil*
1 small onion, peeled and scored in the end
1 celery stalk, minced
½ cup raisins, minced
1 small onion, minced
2 tablespoons Fiesta Brand® Chili Powder
1 tablespoon cumin powder
1 tablespoon lime juice
2 teaspoons salt
½ tablespoon minced garlic
2 teaspoons Fiesta Brand® Black Pepper
1 teaspoon Fiesta Brand® Oregano
1 dried ancho chile, seeded and chopped

Use this method to prepare pork for a variety of dishes such as pork tacos, burritos and much, much more.

Heat a small amount of oil in the bottom of a large pot and brown sides of meat. Add in remaining ingredients along with enough water to cover roast; cover. Cook until meat pulls away from bone or shreds with a fork. You can boil down the water if you want or reserve it for stock. Use the meat in tacos, tamales, burritos and more.

*For a healthier alternative, you can use Texas Pecan Oil.

Ancho chile is a broad, dried chile 3 to 4 inches long and deep reddish brown. It ranges in flavor from mild to pungent. The rich, slightly fruit-flavored ancho is the sweetest of the dried chiles. In its fresh, green state, the ancho is called a poblano chile.

Spicy Apricot Pork

2 to 3 pork steaks (or 4 boneless pork loin chops)
1 teaspoon oil*
1 can chicken stock
3 tablespoons apricot preserves
½ tablespoon hot sauce
1 cup sliced onion

1 garlic clove, minced
1 teaspoon ginger
1 teaspoon coriander
1 teaspoon cumin
1 teaspoon Fiesta Brand® Chili Powder
Flour
2 to 3 cups cooked rice

Heat oil in a large skillet and brown pork. Add chicken stock and remaining ingredients, except flour and rice; simmer until pork is done. Remove pork from skillet and add 1 or 2 tablespoons flour. Stir to make a sauce. Serve pork over rice topped with sauce.

*For a healthier alternative, you can use Texas Pecan Oil.

TEXAS STEAK COOK-OFF, BEEF SYMPOSIUM & TOURIST TRAP

Hico • May

Average attendance over the past four years has increased from approximately 4,000 to more than 6,000 people spending a spectacular day feasting on steaks, listening to live country music, visiting with local artists, "Very interesting chefs" competing for the title of the Best Rib-Eye Steak cooked in Texas, enjoying Texas wines, and taking in the sights of historic Hico, Texas.

254.485.2020 • www.texassteakcookoff.com

Pork Kabobs

2 pounds boneless pork, cubed
1 can pineapple chunks
½ cup soy sauce
2 teaspoons ginger
2 tablespoons salad oil* or Italian
   dressing

1 tablespoon sugar
2 medium onions
1 each green, red and yellow bell pepper
1 can water chestnuts
Salt and Fiesta Brand® Black Pepper

Poke each piece of pork with a fork several times and place in bowl. Cover with juice from pineapples (reserve pineapple chunks), soy sauce, ginger, salad oil and sugar; mix well and set aside to marinate for 1 hour. While meat is marinating, peel onion and chop into large pieces. Wash, stem, and core peppers and cut into large pieces. Open and drain water chestnuts. Alternate meat, onion, peppers and water chestnuts on kabob sticks. (I find it best to use a small, sharp-tipped knife to make a hole in the water chestnut slices before placing on the kabob stick.) Grill over medium-high heat. Season to taste with salt and pepper before serving.

*For a healthier alternative, you can use Texas Pecan Oil.

Trail Riders Barbecue Coffee Pork Butt

1 pork butt or pork roast
½ cup brewed coffee
½ cup barbecue sauce
3 tablespoons mustard
2 tablespoons apple vinegar
1 tablespoon Fiesta Brand® Chili Powder
Salt and Fiesta Brand® Black Pepper to taste

Place pork in large bowl. Combine remaining ingredients, pour over pork, and marinate pork as long as possible. Cook over hot coals or on your covered gas or charcoal grill using medium-high heat. Wrap gently with foil if edges start to burn. When done, chop with a knife and sprinkle with pepper. Serve hot with your favorite sides.

TEXAS BAR-B-Q FESTIVAL

Last weekend in April • Vidor

Vidor Chamber of Commerce has sponsored the festival for almost 30 years. It features good country family fun like a treasure hunt, live entertainment, barbecue cook-off, food and craft vendors, classic car show, carnival rides and games. There are games like Washer Boards and Horse Shoes and a Car Bash, we also have a Doggie "Pageant" and "Parade", all fun and all to support local charities. Join us; you'll be glad you did.

409.769.6339 • www.vidorchamber.com

Spicy-Apple-Glazed Pork Butt

1 (4-pound) pork roast or butt
¼ cup apple juice
2 teaspoons Fiesta Brand® Black Pepper
1 teaspoon salt
3 tablespoons brown sugar
1½ teaspoons ginger
½ cup apple sauce
2 tablespoons lemon juice
1 tablespoon hot sauce
1 teaspoon cumin powder
1 teaspoon thyme
1 teaspoon Fiesta Brand® Cilantro

Place pork roast in a covered container. Combine remaining ingredients and evenly coat pork. Cover and chill overnight, if possible. Save marinade, boil for a basting sauce. Cook pork on a covered grill or smoker at 400° for 1 hour over direct heat. Turn often to prevent burning. Remove from heat, baste and wrap tightly in foil. Move to a cooler part of the grill, or reduce heat, and continue to cook, turning as needed. Use your heat thermometer to check for doneness. Remove from foil, chop or shred and serve hot.

Tex-Mex Pork Burgers

1½ pounds ground pork (can use ¾ pound
    pork and ¾ pound beef)
1 egg
½ cup crushed tortilla chips
½ cup finely chopped onions

1 can green chiles
½ tablespoon Fiesta Brand® Chili Powder
Salt and Fiesta Brand® Black Pepper
½ tablespoon minced garlic
½ cup shredded Cheddar cheese

Combine all ingredients and mix well. Form into equal-sized patties and grill, bake or pan-cook until done. Serve hot on toasted Texas toast with all of your favorite toppings.

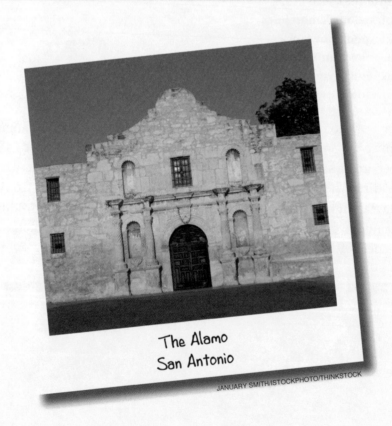

The Alamo
San Antonio

Texas Longhorn Tailgate Brats

12 bratwurst
1 bottle Lone Star beer
½ cup honey
½ tablespoon Fiesta Brand® Chili Powder
½ tablespoon hot sauce
1 large onion, sliced
1 large green pepper, sliced
Texas toast
Barbecue sauce

In a large foil pan, combine brats, beer, honey, chili powder, hot sauce, onion and peppers. Add water to cover brats. Place pan on grill and simmer until veggies are tender and brats begin to plump. Remove brats from juice and place on grill. Cook evenly until all sides are golden brown with grill marks. Lightly toast slices of Texas toast on grill. Serve brats on toast topped with veggies and barbecue sauce.

D. "LONGHORN" CAMPBELL, GALVESTON

Chorizo Sausage

2 pounds ground pork
½ pound ground beef
¼ cup red wine vinegar
2 tablespoons each Fiesta Brand® Chili Powder and Fiesta Brand® Oregano
1 tablespoon minced garlic
1 tablespoon Fiesta Brand® Paprika
1½ teaspoons each salt and Fiesta Brand® Black Pepper
1 teaspoon honey
½ teaspoon ground cumin
Dash lime or lemon juice

Combine all ingredients in a bowl and mix well. Cover tightly and refrigerate at least 1 hour. Form into patties or links and cook as normal. Large links can be grilled and served on a bun.

Quick Pepper Jack Barbecue Ham Hoagies

½ cup barbecue sauce
1 tablespoon mustard
Garlic salt to taste
2 tablespoons minced onion

1 pound deli-shaved ham
Several slices pepper jack cheese
French rolls

In a saucepan over medium heat, combine all ingredients. Stir and heat until cheese is melted and ham is evenly coated. Serve hot on French rolls.

Peppered Ham Steaks and Gravy

2 thick-cut ham steaks
Oil*
Fiesta Brand® Black Pepper to taste
1 tablespoon minced garlic
3 tablespoons minced onion
2 tablespoons parsley
2 tablespoons vinegar
3 tablespoons soy sauce
Water
Flour

Cook steaks in a hot skillet with some oil. Add black pepper, garlic, onion, parsley, vinegar and soy sauce while ham is cooking. Turn to cook other side. Remove steaks to a plate. Add a few spoonfuls of water and flour to drippings in the skillet. Cook and stir adding water and/or flour until you have desired thickness for gravy. Spoon over top of ham steaks and serve immediately.

*For a healthier alternative, you can use Texas Pecan Oil.

Grilled Ham and Taters

2 cups cooked chopped ham
1 (32-ounce) package frozen hash browns
1 bell pepper, chopped
1 sweet onion, finely chopped
2 teaspoons Fiesta Brand® Crushed Red Pepper
2 teaspoons Fiesta Brand® Paprika
1 teaspoon salt
½ teaspoon Fiesta Brand® Black Pepper
1 can cream of chicken soup
1 (12-ounce) can evaporated milk
2 cups grated Cheddar cheese, divided

Mix all ingredients, except 1 cup grated cheese, in a large foil pan coated with nonstick spray. Cover with foil and place on rack of a covered grill. Allow to cook using medium heat until everything is warmed and edges are beginning to brown. Uncover and top with cheese. Return to grill until cheese is melted; serve.

Sauces, Gravies, Marinades & Rubs

Taco Sauce, page 157

Vera Cruz Sauce

½ cup olive oil, divided*
1 garlic clove, minced
¼ cup finely chopped onion
2 cans stewed tomatoes
2 teaspoons Fiesta Brand® Garlic Powder
1 tablespoon Fiesta Brand® Oregano
1 tablespoon capers
2 jalapeño peppers, seeded and chopped
5 green olives, coarsely chopped
¼ cup water
Salt to taste

Warm ¼ cup oil in a medium saucepan. Sauté garlic and onion until soft. Add tomatoes and cook over low heat about 10 minutes. Add remaining ingredients including remaining ¼ cup olive oil. Simmer an additional 20 minutes.

*For a healthier alternative, you can use Texas Pecan Oil instead of olive oil.

Enchilada Brown Sauce

½ stick butter*
4 tablespoons flour
1 teaspoon Fiesta Brand® Chili Powder
1 teaspoon Fiesta Brand® Garlic Powder

1 teaspoon Fiesta Brand® Black Pepper
½ teaspoon salt
1 can beef stock

Melt butter in a hot skillet; add flour. Stir until flour begins to brown. Reduce heat and add remaining ingredients. Cook over low heat for 20 minutes stirring as needed.

*For a healthier alternative, you can use Texas Pecan Oil instead of butter.

Waterfall at Zilker Park
Austin

ENDI DEWATA/ISTOCKPHOTO/THINKSTOCK

Wasabi Sauce

1¼ cups white wine
2 tablespoons white wine vinegar
¼ cup finely chopped onion
2 teaspoons minced garlic
1 tablespoon Fiesta Brand® Cilantro
1 stick butter*
1 tablespoon wasabi paste
1 tablespoon soy sauce
1 tablespoon olive oil*
2 teaspoons cumin powder
½ teaspoon Fiesta Brand® Ground Italian Spice Blend
  (Italian seasoning)
Dash salt and Fiesta Brand® Black Pepper
3 tablespoons sour cream

Combine wine, vinegar, onions and garlic in a saucepan over medium heat. Reduce to half. Add remaining ingredients except sour cream and stir. Remove from heat and add sour cream when cooled. Stir to mix; chill and serve.

*For a healthier alternative, you can use Texas Pecan Oil instead of olive oil.

TEXAS HILL COUNTRY WINE AND FOOD FESTIVAL

April • Austin

For 23 years, the Texas Hill Country Wine and Food Festival has been the state's premier wine and food event. The annual four-day festival, held in April, attracts thousands who come to celebrate Texas' multi-cultural culinary and viticultural achievements in its vibrant capital, Austin. The festival features winemakers and chefs from Texas, America and beyond, and remains true to its mission to celebrate the rich traditions that influence Texas wine and food.

512.249.6300
hillcountrywineandmusic.com

Taco Sauce

1 (16-ounce) can tomato sauce
1 teaspoon cumin
½ teaspoon Fiesta Brand® Garlic Powder
2 teaspoons Fiesta Brand® Onion Powder
½ teaspoon Fiesta Brand® Oregano
½ teaspoon Worcestershire sauce
Dash sugar
Dash Fiesta Brand® Cayenne Pepper
Salt and Fiesta Brand® Black Pepper to taste

Combine all ingredients in a small bowl. Chill and serve.

Spicy Ketchup

A fun twist on regular ketchup. Just mix, blend and serve.

1 cup ketchup
1 cup medium salsa
2 tablespoons hot sauce
½ tablespoon Fiesta Brand® Cilantro
1 teaspoon ground cumin
1 teaspoon Fiesta Brand® Onion Powder

Use a blender to blend into a smooth sauce. Add a bit of water if needed to make thinner. Chill, covered, overnight or for as long as possible (up to 3 days) before using.

Texas-Style Steak Sauce

½ cup butter, melted*
½ cup Worcestershire sauce
½ tablespoon Fiesta Brand® Black Pepper
½ tablespoon hot sauce
Juice from 1 lemon
1 tablespoon mustard
½ tablespoon minced garlic
1 teaspoon soy sauce
Salt and pepper
1 teaspoon flour
Minced jalapeño pepper to taste (optional)

Combine all ingredients in a saucepan and stir over medium heat until butter melts. Cover and chill an hour or longer before serving.

*For a healthier alternative, you can use Texas Pecan Oil instead of butter.

For those times when steak sauce in a bottle just will not do.

WORLD CHAMPIONSHIP FIDDLERS' FESTIVAL & STEAK COOK-OFF

June • Crockett

Crockett, Texas, is home to the World Champion Fiddlers' Festival. Starting in 1936, we boast 72 years of World Class Fiddlin' for all ages. The day ends with the Regional Steak Cook-Off, where the winners are offered a chance to compete in the World Championship Cook-Off. Join in a wonderful weekend of old-time music and fiddlin' fun.

1.888.269.2359
www.crockettareachamber.org

Barbecue Sauce

¼ pound butter*
1 cup vinegar
1 sour pickle, finely chopped
2 tablespoons chopped onion
2 tablespoons Worcestershire sauce
2 tablespoons chili sauce
4 slices lemon
1 teaspoon brown sugar
1 green pepper, finely chopped

Combine all ingredients and mix thoroughly. Place in a saucepan on a slow fire and cook until butter melts, stirring constantly. Place on top of a double boiler and keep warm until ready to use on meats or as a sauce for sandwiches.

*For a healthier alternative, you can use Texas Pecan Oil instead of butter.

HOT DIGGITY HOG FEST

Green or Red Chili Sauce

2 pounds red or green chiles
2 garlic cloves, minced
½ teaspoon cumin powder
½ teaspoon Fiesta Brand® Chili
    Powder
2 teaspoons lemon or lime juice

1 teaspoon salt
2 tablespoons oil*
1 jalapeño pepper, seeded and
    diced
2 tablespoons water

Bake chiles in oven on 450° until they begin to turn brown. Remove and allow to cool slightly. Remove seeds and stems. Blend everything in a food processor until almost smooth. Don't puree. Chill and serve.

*For a healthier alternative, you can use Texas Pecan Oil.

Black Gold Barbecue Sauce

1 cup ketchup
1 cup coffee
¼ cup orange juice
1 tablespoon Worcestershire sauce
⅓ cup minced onion
2 teaspoons Fiesta Brand® Garlic Powder
1 teaspoon salt
Dash hot sauce

Texas is famous for black gold. Oil that is. This barbecue sauce does not call for oil, but it does have plenty of flavor.

Combine everything in a bowl and mix. Chill before using.

CHISHOLM TRAIL ROUNDUP BBQ & MUSIC FESTIVAL

Lockhart • 2nd week in June

This annual 3-day arts and crafts and music festival is hosted by the Lockhart Chamber of Commerce. You'll enjoy a parade, Chuckwagon Breakfast, BBQ and Chili Cook-Offs, live music, dancing, food and fun. There is also a carnival and Coronation of the Queens Court. Join us for good family fun in the BBQ Capital of Texas.

512.398.2818
www.chisholmtrailroundup.com

Tequila Barbecue Sauce

⅓ cup tequila
½ cup Worcestershire sauce
½ cup soy sauce
¼ cup steak sauce
½ cup pineapple juice

2 tablespoons minced onion
1 tablespoon minced garlic
1 tablespoon lemon juice
1 teaspoon salt
1 teaspoon Fiesta Brand® Black Pepper

Combine all ingredients in a saucepan and simmer about 30 minutes. Chill before serving.

Lone Star Mustard Basting Sauce

⅓ cup mustard powder
1 tablespoon horseradish
1 Lone Star beer
½ cup ketchup
½ tablespoon tarragon or thyme

2 tablespoons vinegar
¼ cup brown sugar
¼ cup minced onion
½ tablespoon Fiesta Brand® Chili Powder

Combine everything in a saucepan and simmer over medium heat about 35 minutes.

White Texas Gravy

½ cup meat drippings (can use shortening but drippings are much better)
¼ cup minced onion
1½ cups flour
1 teaspoon garlic salt
1 teaspoon Fiesta Brand® Black Pepper
8 ounces evaporated milk
1 cup water

This version of white gravy is by-far my hands-down favorite. I think you will enjoy it as well.

In a skillet, heat drippings until hot. Add onion and flour a little a time stirring constantly until brown. Add remaining ingredients. Remove from heat and stir while gravy thickens.

White Sweet Gravy

1 stick butter*
2 tablespoons bacon or sausage grease
Flour
Milk
3 teaspoons sugar or honey
1½ teaspoons Fiesta Brand® Black Pepper

In a skillet, melt butter and grease. Add flour and milk to desired consistency, stirring constantly. Add sugar and pepper continuing to stir.

*For a healthier alternative, you can use Texas Pecan Oil instead of butter.

Beef and Rib Rub

1 tablespoon Fiesta Brand® Garlic Powder
1 tablespoon Fiesta Brand® Onion Powder
1 tablespoon salt
1 tablespoon Fiesta Brand® Cayenne Pepper
1 tablespoon Fiesta Brand® Black Pepper
½ cup brown sugar
½ cup Fiesta Brand® Paprika
2 teaspoons cumin powder

Mix all ingredients together and use as needed. Store in a shaker. Rub or sprinkle on meat. Double as needed.

Lemon Pepper Ginger Rub

1 tablespoon Fiesta Brand® Lemon Pepper
1 tablespoon Fiesta Brand® Garlic Powder
1 tablespoon Fiesta Brand® Paprika
½ tablespoon salt
½ tablespoon ginger

Mix all ingredients together and use as needed. Store in a shaker. Rub or sprinkle on meat. Double as needed.

Steak Rub

1 tablespoon Fiesta Brand® Black Pepper
1 tablespoon salt
1 tablespoon parsley
½ tablespoon Fiesta Brand® Garlic Powder

Mix all ingredients together; rub into meat before cooking. Make larger quantities by using 2 parts pepper, salt, and parsley to 1 part garlic powder; store in a shaker and use as needed.

Homemade Taco Seasoning

6 teaspoons Fiesta Brand® Chili Powder
5 teaspoons Fiesta Brand® Paprika
4½ teaspoons cumin
3 teaspoons Fiesta Brand® Onion Powder
2½ teaspoons Fiesta Brand® Garlic Powder
⅛ teaspoon Fiesta Brand® Cayenne Pepper
1 teaspoon salt (optional)

Combine all ingredients and use as you would pre-packaged taco seasoning.

Poultry

Chicken Mole Tex-Mex, page 168

CLEAR CREEK
709 Harris Avenue • Kemah, Texas 77565

Winery: 281-334-8300
www.clearcreekvineyard.com

Clipper House Inn: 281-334-2517
www.clipperhouseinn.com

Eculent: 713-429-4311
www.eculent.com

CLEAR CREEK
WINERY • VINEYARD • RESORT

Clear Creek Winery, Vineyard & Resort is definitely a destination not to be missed when visiting South Texas.

Nestled in the heart of Kemah (30 minutes South of Houston), Clear Creek features the quaint **Clipper House Inn** with seven romantic cottages surrounding the winery's manicured gardens and vineyards.

The cottages are original 1930's bungalows filled with antiques from the owner's world travels. Each cottage is named after a famous clipper ship befitting the design of the cottage interior and features plush beds with luxurious linens, pristine private bathrooms, flat screen televisions, and cozy sitting areas.

Clear Creek is also home to **Eculent**, the only total immersion restaurant in America where the sights, sounds, and smells are orchestrated to match the food. Eculent features three distinct menus; a vegetarian, gluten-free menu utilizing the restaurant's own aeroponic gardens, a Texas-only menu featuring the best and often unknown products from the great State of Texas, and finally a chef's tasting menu designed around the culinary team's most creative thoughts.

Of course no trip to Clear Creek would be complete without trying the award-winning wines. **The winery** is known for its handcrafted sweet fruit wines and full-bodied dry wines.

The Peach Chardonnay or Strawberry Zinfandel, both of which won double Gold medals are perfect for warm Summer days while the barrel-aged reserve wines like Malbec or Cabernet Franc are perfectly paired with a great Texas steak.

Clear Creek offers something for everyone and should be at the top of your list of places to visit when in Texas.

Blackberry Merlot Chicken

1 pint blackberries, freshly rinsed
1 cup Clear Creek Blackberry Merlot Wine
Salt
1 tablespoon white wine vinegar
2 large (12 ounces) sweet potatoes
4 (4- to 6-ounce) chicken breasts, skin on
White pepper
9 tablespoons unsalted butter, divided
5 ounces heavy cream
6 ounces baby zucchini, diced
6 ounces baby yellow summer squash, diced
Olive oil

Start off with your most time consuming preparation—the sauce. In a small sauce-pot add blackberries and wine. Bring to just below a simmer, for a slow reduction. Season to taste with salt. Reduce wine to half, berries should be cooked and macerated. Add vinegar and remove from heat; set aside to cool.

While blackberry sauce is reducing, peel and small dice the sweet potatoes. Put in small pot, cover with salted water, and bring to a boil. Boil until soft and tender, about 10 minutes.

While sweet potatoes are boiling, Purée blackberry sauce (that has now cooled to warm) in a food processor or blender, then pass through a fine strainer. Return the seed-free velvety liquid to its sauce-pot and reserve.

Heat a cast-iron skillet to medium-high heat. Season chicken breasts with salt and pepper. Lightly oil skillet and sear chicken breasts, skin side down, until golden and crispy. Flip and finish on low in skillet with a lid, or in oven at 325°, to internal temperature of 165° to 170°.

While chicken is finishing, pass the cooked sweet potatoes through a ricer or tami. Gently warm 6 tablespoons butter and heavy cream together and stir into sweet potato. Season with salt and white pepper to desired taste.

Remove chicken from skillet; allow to rest before slicing. Sauté zucchini and yellow squash over high heat with a light coating of oil, salt and pepper. Warm blackberry sauce on low heat; mount with 3 tablespoons butter.

Plate artistically. Makes 4 servings.

CLEAR CREEK WINERY, VINEYARD & RESORT

Chicken Mole Tex-Mex

4 cups water
2 to 3 whole chickens, cut-up
1 celery stalk, minced
3 tablespoons Fiesta Brand® Cilantro
Salt and Fiesta Brand® Black Pepper to taste
1 teaspoon ground cumin
1 teaspoon Fiesta Brand® Ground Cloves
2 tablespoons Fiesta Brand® Chili Powder
1 tablespoon minced garlic
¼ cup raisins
¼ cup crushed tortilla chips
1 jalapeño pepper, seeds removed
⅓ cup chopped onion
1 tablespoon olive oil*
1 can tomato soup
1 ounce unsweetened chocolate, melted
¼ cup slivered almonds, toasted

Bring water, chicken and celery to a boil in a large pot. Cover and reduce heat, letting chicken simmer about 1½ hours. Remove chicken from broth, pull chicken meat from bones and set aside to cool. Strain broth keeping liquid. In a blender, combine half the broth with cilantro, salt, pepper, cumin, cloves, chili powder, garlic, raisins, tortilla chips, jalapeño and onion. Blend well. Heat olive oil in a skillet and slowly pour in sauce. Continue to cook until hot; add remaining ingredients. When heated through, drizzle over chicken. Serve over rice with vegetables or even tortilla chips.

*For a healthier alternative, you can use Texas Pecan Oil instead of olive oil.

Texas Fried Chicken

STEPHANIE FREY/ISTOCKPHOTO/THINKSTOCK

4 whole chickens, cut-up
3 to 4 cups buttermilk
2 teaspoons hot sauce
1 can green chiles, drained
2 teaspoons each salt and Fiesta Brand®
   Black Pepper
1½ cups all-purpose flour
½ cup cornmeal
½ cup crushed tortilla chips
1½ pounds shortening
2 tablespoons bacon grease

Rinse chicken. Combine buttermilk, hot sauce, chiles, salt and pepper. Add chicken and refrigerate an hour or more. In a paper bag, combine flour, cornmeal and tortilla chips. Add chicken pieces a few at a time and toss to coat evenly. Fry chicken in a hot cast-iron skillet with shortening and bacon grease. Turn as few times as possible. Cook until golden, drain on a paper towel, serve hot.

Paula's Quick and Easy Chicken Breasts with Fresh Mozzarella

4 skinless boneless chicken breasts (1½ pounds total)
Salt to taste
Freshly ground Fiesta Brand® Black Pepper to taste
2 tablespoons unsalted butter*
1 garlic clove
½ cup white wine
1 (8-ounce) fresh mozzarella roll, cut into ¼-inch slices
4 sprigs fresh tarragon

Season chicken breasts with salt and pepper. Melt butter in a large skillet over medium heat. Add garlic and chicken breasts and sauté 6 to 10 minutes, or until golden brown on both sides, turning as necessary. Remove to a plate and keep warm. Deglaze pan with wine and simmer briefly to reduce to half its original volume. Return chicken to skillet and cook 1 minute. Place 2 slices fresh mozzarella on top of each chicken breast and place 1 sprig tarragon on top. Cover pan and remove from heat. Set aside in a warm place for a few minutes and let mozzarella soften and begin to melt. Sprinkle with additional salt and/or pepper, as desired. Remove garlic before serving. To serve, spoon some of the sauce over breast. Serves 4.

*For a healthier alternative, you can use Texas Pecan Oil instead of butter.

PAULA LAMBERT
THE CHEESE LOVER'S COOKBOOK AND GUIDE
SUBMITTED BY GRAPEFEST

BEAUJOLAIS WINE FESTIVAL
Third Friday in November • Dallas

France Meets Texas at the annual Beaujolais Wine Festival hosted by The French-American Chamber of Commerce Dallas/Fort Worth. Held at the World Trade Center in Dallas, this unforgettable evening includes a commemorative wine glass, food and wine tasting, fashion show, blind wine tasting, silent auction and more. You won't want to miss the "Battle of the Bottle" wine tasting featuring French and Texas wines, sampling some of Dallas' best restaurants' specialties, and many more surprises.

972.241.0111 • www.faccdallas.com

Roasted Chicken

1 (3- to 5-pound) whole chicken
1 tablespoon butter, softened*
¾ teaspoon salt
½ teaspoon Fiesta Brand® Black Pepper
¼ teaspoon thyme
1 head garlic (yes, a whole head of garlic)
½ cup chicken broth or water
¼ cup white wine

Remove thawed chicken from refrigerator 30 minutes before baking; rinse with water and pat dry. Preheat oven to 400°. Rub chicken with softened butter. Sprinkle with salt, pepper and thyme. Place in a cast-iron skillet and roast 40 to 45 minutes for 3 pounds, about 1 hour for 5 pounds. Immediately after placing chicken in oven, peel outer skin from head of garlic, place in small (about 2-cup size) baking dish, add ½ cup chicken broth or water, cover, and bake in oven with chicken. When chicken is done (I check by cutting into joint of thigh to body of chicken or the wing joint), transfer to a platter and keep warm. Squeeze garlic from skins and mash with fork. In skillet that chicken was cooked, skim off some of the chicken fat from the broth, add wine, whisk in garlic, boil 2 minutes scraping browned bits from bottom and sides of skillet. Cut off portions of chicken and spoon broth mixture on top. It is not too much garlic. This is the best chicken recipe I have.

*For a healthier alternative, you can use Texas Pecan Oil instead of butter.

SANDRA K. FITE, GILMER

Margarita Chicken Quarters

4 whole chicken legs quarters
6 teaspoons cooking oil*
½ cup liquid margarita mix
¼ cup lime juice
2 teaspoons Fiesta Brand® Chili Powder

2 teaspoons cumin powder
1 teaspoon ground coriander
¼ teaspoon Fiesta Brand® Cayenne Pepper
Salt and Fiesta Brand® Black Pepper

Wash chicken well. Mix oil, margarita mix, lime juice, chili powder, cumin, coriander, cayenne pepper, salt and pepper. Add chicken and marinate an hour or longer. Bake at 350° about 45 minutes on a treated pan or cooking dish. Before removing from oven, broil about 2 minutes to brown, if needed. Adjust cooking time based on size of chicken quarters. Serve hot.

*For a healthier alternative, you can use Texas Pecan Oil.

Dallas

JEREMY EDWARDS/ ISTOCKPHOTO/THINKSTOCK

George's Dancing Texas Chicken

2 whole fryer chickens
Fiesta Brand® Lemon Pepper
½ can beer

George calls this his dancing chicken recipe because you know the chicken is done when the wings raise up.. "Like it's dancing!"

Clean chickens and remove excess fat. Coat chicken with lemon pepper seasoning (or your favorite seasoning). Place a half-full can of beer in the opening on the bottom of the chicken and place the whole chicken (standing up) on the grill using the legs and the can to balance. Use a toothpick to fold neck skin over to seal top of chicken. Grill on medium heat until chicken juices run clear. The wings should be hanging down when you start. As the skin cooks, it will draw up and the arms will rise. Serve hot.

GEORGE EAGER, BOERNE

Easy Chicken Cheese Enchiladas

1 envelope taco seasoning mix

1 tablespoon olive oil*

1 cup water

1 pound boneless skinless chicken
    breasts, sliced

⅓ cup chopped fresh cilantro

½ teaspoon salt

1 can green chiles

1 jar salsa

6 to 8 flour tortillas

1 container ricotta cheese

2 cups shredded Monterey Jack cheese

In a skillet, combine first 8 ingredients and cook until chicken is done. Working quickly, remove skillet from heat and spoon equal amounts into flour tortillas adding a spoonful of ricotta cheese. Leave as much juice/sauce/drippings in the skillet as possible. Place wrapped and filled tortillas in a treated glass baking dish. Spoon skillet juice over top. Top with cheese and bake at 350° until cheese is melted.

*For a healthier alternative, you can use Texas Pecan Oil instead of olive oil.

LESLIE ELIEFF/ISTOCKPHOTO/THINKSTOCK

Chicken Bombs

5 boneless, skinless chicken breasts
5 jalapeño peppers
4 ounces cream cheese, softened
1 cup grated Colby Jack cheese
20 strips bacon
1 cup BBQ sauce
Salt and pepper to taste
2 tablespoons Texas Pecan Oil

Slice chicken breasts in half width-wise (each half will make 1 Chicken Bomb). Place between two pieces of wax paper and pound to ¼-inch thickness. Rub with pecan oil and season each with salt and pepper. Slice jalapeños in half LENGTH wise and remove seeds, ribs and the end with the stem. In a small bowl, mix softened cream cheese with Colby Jack. Fill each jalapeño half with about 1 tablespoon cheese mixture. Place 1 jalapeño half at the end of each pounded breast piece. Roll over and together. *It doesn't always close the way you think it should. No worries! The bacon will pull it all together. Wrap each breast piece with 2 slices bacon. I do 1 at a time (obviously), and just sort of wrap tightly and tuck the ends of the bacon under the strips.

Preheat grill to 350°. Cook over indirect heat 20 to 25 minutes, turning every 4 to 5 minutes. Baste chicken with BBQ sauce each time you turn it. Giving it one final basting right before it's done. Chicken is ready when it reaches an internal temp of 165°. If you don't have a meat thermometer, pierce chicken with a fork. If juices run clear, it's done. If you prefer to use the oven, bake at 375°, uncovered, for 30 minutes. Baste with BBQ sauce a few times during cooking. Baste once again when finished, and place under broil setting for a few minutes so bacon can crisp completely.

TEXAS PECAN RANCH • WWW.TEXASPECANRANCH.COM

Chicken Tacos with Lime Sauce

4 cups cooked and shredded chicken
   (about 3 chicken breasts)
2 tablespoons oil*
1½ cups salsa
2 tablespoons Fiesta Brand®
   Chili Powder
½ tablespoon cumin powder

Salt, Fiesta Brand® Black Pepper and
   Fiesta Brand® Garlic Powder to taste
½ tablespoon Fiesta Brand® Cilantro
Shredded lettuce
Shredded cabbage
1 cup shredded Cheddar cheese
10 to 12 soft or crunchy taco shells

Lime Sauce:

1 cup mayonnaise
½ cup sour cream
3 tablespoons lime juice

Dash Fiesta Brand® Chili Powder
Dash parsley

In a skillet, combine chicken, oil, salsa, chili powder, cumin, salt, pepper, garlic powder and cilantro. Cook over medium heat until well-heated; remove from heat. In a bowl, combine Lime Sauce ingredients; mix well and chill until needed. Place desired amount of heated chicken mixture into a shell, top with Lime Sauce, cabbage, lettuce, cheese and any of your favorite toppings. Serve hot with rice and beans.

*For a healthier alternative, you can use Texas Pecan Oil.

Chicken Flautas

3 cups cooked, shredded chicken
2 cans tomato soup
1 cup shredded Cheddar cheese
1 envelope taco seasoning

1 can black beans, drained and rinsed
Oil for frying*
12 to 14 corn tortillas
Lettuce, sour cream, and guacamole

Combine chicken, soup, cheese, seasoning and beans in a saucepan; cook over medium heat until thick. Spoon equal amounts into corn tortillas and roll tightly. These should be as thick as a flute. Fry in hot oil until golden and serve hot topped with lettuce, sour cream and guacamole.

*For a healthier alternative, you can use Texas Pecan Oil.

Tex-Mex Seasoned Chicken Pasta

3 cups chicken, cubed
2 teaspoons Fiesta Brand® Cajun-All
2 teaspoons Fiesta Brand® Chili Powder
1 teaspoon cumin powder
1 teaspoon thyme
2 tablespoons butter*
1 green chile, minced
1 red bell pepper, diced
1 small can chopped mushrooms, drained

⅓ cup chopped onion
1 cup heavy cream
¼ teaspoon Fiesta Brand® Cilantro
¼ teaspoon Fiesta Brand® Lemon Pepper
¼ teaspoon salt
⅛ teaspoon Fiesta Brand® Black Pepper
⅛ teaspoon Fiesta Brand® Garlic Powder
4 ounces linguini, cooked and drained
Parmesan cheese, grated

Rinse chicken and set aside. In a bowl, combine Cajun seasoning, chili powder, cumin and thyme. Coat each piece of chicken with mixture. In a large skillet, over medium heat, sauté chicken in butter until tender. Add green chiles, bell pepper, mushrooms and onions; continue to cook 2 to 3 minutes. Reduce heat to low; gently stir in cream, cilantro, lemon pepper, salt, pepper, garlic powder and linguini. Stir well and continue to cook until everything is heated through. Sprinkle with Parmesan cheese. Serve hot.

*For a healthier alternative, you can use Texas Pecan Oil instead of butter.

Smoked Duck Polenta with Blackberry Herb Sauce

1¼ quarts vegetable or chicken stock
½ teaspoon salt
½ pound polenta
1 ounce butter*
2 ounces Parmesan cheese
1 pound smoked duck breast, cut into small dice
2 tablespoons each fresh chives, parsley and rosemary

Bring stock and salt to a boil in a heavy pot. Add polenta in a thin stream, stirring constantly. Reduce heat to low and cook, stirring occasionally, about 15 to 20 minutes. Remove from heat and add remaining ingredients; set aside to cool. Refrigerate at least 8 hours. Cut polenta into shape and grill on a medium-hot grill until heated through. Serve with Blackberry Herb Sauce. Serves 8 to 10.

Blackberry Herb Sauce:

½ pound fresh blackberries
4 ounces water
4 to 6 ounces sugar, depending on sweetness of berries
3 tablespoons cornstarch, mixed with cold water
Juice from 1 lemon
3 tablespoons finely chopped fresh rosemary

Mix first 3 ingredients together in pot, bring to a boil. Thicken with cornstarch, purée and strain. Add lemon juice and rosemary.

*For a healthier alternative, you can use Texas Pecan Oil instead of butter.

CHEF KEITH JONES (THE CHAMPAGNE CHEF)
SUBMITTED BY GRAPEFEST

Thanksgiving Leftover Turkey Nachos

½ pound leftover roast turkey meat, shredded
1½ tablespoons lemon juice
2 tablespoons vegetable oil*
1 red bell pepper, chopped
1 yellow bell pepper, chopped
1 garlic clove, finely chopped
½ teaspoon cumin
1 teaspoon Fiesta Brand® Ground Italian Spice Blend (Italian seasoning)
1 can black beans, drained and rinsed
1 can whole-kernel corn, drained
1 large bag tortilla chips
2 cups grated jalapeño jack cheese
¼ cup chopped onion (optional)
½ cup chopped fresh cilantro (optional)
1 cup sour cream (optional)
2 jalapeño peppers, sliced (optional)

Preheat oven to 350°. Combine turkey with lemon juice; set aside. Heat oil in a skillet and sauté bell peppers and garlic with cumin and Italian seasoning. Stir in beans and corn. Add turkey. Mix well and cook just until heated through (do not overcook). Using a large pan or oven-safe dish, layer chips, meat mixture and cheese; repeat. Bake at 350° until cheese is melted. Top with onions, cilantro, sour cream and jalapeños before serving, if desired.

*For a healthier alternative, you can use Texas Pecan Oil.

Spicy Onion Turkey Legs

4 to 6 turkey legs
½ stick melted butter*
2 tablespoons hot sauce
1 teaspoon Fiesta Brand® Garlic Powder
1 teaspoon Fiesta Brand® Chili Powder
1 envelope dry onion soup mix
Lemon juice

Brush turkey legs with butter and hot sauce. Sprinkle with garlic powder, chili powder and onion soup mix. Drizzle with lemon juice and grill over medium heat or bake at 375° (about 30 minutes) until juices run clear and meat is fully cooked and golden. Wrap edges with foil if they brown too quickly. Serve hot.

*For a healthier alternative, you can use Texas Pecan Oil instead of butter.

Fish & Seafood

Campfire Honey-Butter Fillets, page 185

We always hear from people who ask us . . .
"How do I use Pecan Oil?"

Our answer is simple; use it just like you would olive oil or butter.

As a matter of fact, pecan oil is a great substitute for both of those fats to use in your everyday cooking. Pecan oil has a very subtle nutty flavor and some say it has no flavor at all! This is a great advantage for those who want to taste the flavor and seasoning of the food they are cooking as olive oil has a very distinct taste and butter, even though it tastes great, it's very fattening.

Four things make pecan oil a superior cooking oil:

Light Neutral Flavor • Low in Saturated Fat • High Smoke Point • Long Shelf Life

Texas Pecan Oil has only 9.5% saturated fat compared to Olive Oil with 13.5%, Peanut Oil with 16.9%, Corn Oil with 12.7%, and Butter with a whopping 66% saturated fat.

Texas Pecan Oil has over 90% unsaturated fatty acids with almost equal components of monounsaturated (52%) & polyunsaturated (38.5%) providing a great balance between the two.

All of these nutritional factors combine to make Texas Pecan Oil the most heart-healthy oil available, while maintaining great flavor, color, and quality.

Texas Pecan Ranch
Houston, Texas
www.texaspecanranch.com
(281) 826-1436

Texas Pecan Ranch is a proud member of the GO TEXAN agricultural program.

BBQ Roasted Salmon

¼ cup pineapple juice
2 tablespoons fresh lemon juice
4 (6-ounce) salmon filets
¼ cup Texas Pecan Oil, divided
2 tablespoons brown sugar
4 teaspoons chili powder
2 teaspoons grated lemon rind
¾ teaspoon ground cumin
½ teaspoon salt
¼ teaspoon ground cinnamon
8 thin lemon slices

Combine first 3 ingredients in a zip-top plastic bag; seal and marinate in refrigerator 1 hour, turning occasionally. Preheat oven to 400°. Remove fish from bag; discard marinade. Coat bottom of dish with half of pecan oil. Drizzle remaining pecan oil over fish. Rub pecan oil into the surface to coat.

Combine sugar, chili powder, lemon zest, cumin, salt and cinnamon in a bowl. Rub over fish; place in an 11x7-inch baking dish. Bake at 400° for 12 minutes or until fish flakes easily when tested with a fork. Serve with lemon slices. Serves 4.

TEXAS PECAN RANCH • WWW.TEXASPECANRANCH.COM

Red Snapper El Salsa

4 to 5 red snapper fillets
Juice from 1 lime
¼ cup white wine
Salt to taste
1 tablespoon olive oil*
1½ tablespoon capers
1½ cups salsa
2 jalapeño peppers, seeded and diced
3 tablespoons parsley
1 onion, chopped
1 tablespoon Fiesta Brand® Oregano
2 garlic cloves, minced
1 small can sliced black olives, drained
Salt and Fiesta Brand® Black Pepper to taste

Sprinkle fish fillets with lime juice, white wine and salt. In a skillet over medium-high heat, cook fillets in 1 tablespoon (or more if needed) olive oil. Just before fish is done, add capers and continue to cook until fish is cooked through. Remove fish to a plate; add remaining ingredients to skillet. Stir to mix and serve over fillets when heated through.

*For a healthier alternative, you can use Texas Pecan Oil.

FESTIVAL OF WINE & FOOD
May • Rockport

The Texas Maritime Museum hosts wine tasting, wine seminars, fine foods, and entertainment on the Museum grounds during the popular Festival of Wine & Food. Texas Maritime Museum also created and developed an award-winning cookbook entitled *Marithyme Treasures* in 2001 with Jo Beth Hill, patron and founder of the project. The cookbook won a regional prize from the Tabasco Community Cookbooks Awards and has been showcased by both the NBC TODAY show/Willard Scott and Coastal Living Magazine.

1.866.729.2469 • www.texasfestivalofwines.com

Campfire Honey-Butter Fillets

1 to 2 pounds fish fillets
1 cup milk
1 egg
1 tablespoon honey
1 tablespoon melted butter*
1 teaspoon sugar

1 cup flour
2 tablespoons cornmeal
Salt and Fiesta Brand® Black Pepper
   to taste
Oil for frying*

Rinse fillets and set aside to dry. In a bowl, combine milk, egg, honey, butter and sugar; stir until sugar is dissolved and ingredients are combined well. In a separate bowl, combine flour, cornmeal, salt and pepper. Heat oil in a skillet. Dip a fillet in the honey egg wash then dredge lightly in flour mixture. Repeat, if needed. Place fillet in skillet with hot oil; cook until golden brown. Repeat with remaining fillets.

*For a healthier alternative, you can use Texas Pecan Oil.

Grilled Tuna with Cucumber Yogurt Sauce

2 cups plain yogurt
1 tablespoon lemon juice
2 garlic cloves, minced
1 tablespoon chopped dill
Dash hot sauce

½ cucumber, peeled and diced
1 teaspoon relish
Salt and Fiesta Brand® Black Pepper
6 (8-ounce) tuna steaks
Olive oil*

Combine yogurt with lemon juice, garlic, dill, hot sauce, cucumber, relish and salt and pepper to taste. Cover and chill. Brush tuna steaks with olive oil and sprinkle with salt and pepper to taste. Grill over medium-high heat or broil in the oven 15 to 20 minutes, or until fish flakes easily; turn only once. Serve hot with Cucumber Yogurt Sauce on the side.

*For a healthier alternative, you can use Texas Pecan Oil.

WAYNE SHACKLEFORD, AUSTIN

Cornmeal-Breaded Guadalupe Bass

1 to 2 pounds Guadalupe bass fillets
1 egg
1 cup milk
1 tablespoon Italian dressing
1 box corn muffin mix
1 tablespoon Fiesta Brand® Cajun-All
1 teaspoon cumin powder
1 onion, sliced
1 green bell pepper, sliced

Rinse fillets and set aside to dry. Combine egg, milk and Italian dressing in a bowl. In a separate bowl, combine corn muffin mix, Cajun seasoning and cumin powder. Dip each fillet in egg mixture, then corn muffin mixture. Repeat as needed and pan fry in hot oil along with onion and green pepper slices.

STEVE MEAGON, DALLAS

The official state fish of Texas, Guadalupe Bass are found only in the Lone Star State. Found in Texas' smaller fast-flowing streams, the Guadalupe Bass is not really a bass at all, but is actually a sunfish.

Grilled Catfish ala Mexicana

This entree will take about 2.5 hours from prep to plate but is worth every ounce of effort. The heat level can range from mild to fiery hot depending on how many fresh chilies and variety used.

12 fresh Pequin chiles, crushed
12 fresh garlic cloves, divided
2 to 3 limes, juiced (don't strain; include pulp)
5 tablespoon olive oil, divided
2 large white onions, chopped
3 large jalapeño, seeded and chopped
1 large bell pepper, seeded and chopped
14 ounces all-natural free-range chicken broth
12 fresh Roma tomatoes (2 pounds), blanched, peeled and coarse chopped
½ bunch cilantro, chopped

5 ounces tomato sauce (bottled crushed Roma tomato all-natural from Italy, if available)
4 to 5 teaspoons TSS Southwestern Sizzler
1 teaspoon sea salt
4 ounces soft-melt white cheese, optional
4 catfish fillets
TSS Seasoning for catfish fillets
½ tablespoon real butter
7 stuffed queen olives, sliced (for garnish)
1 jumbo avocado, sliced (for garnish)

Crush Pequins, 3 garlic cloves and some lime juice (to taste) in a molcajete or food processor. Chop remaining 9 cloves garlic. Add olive oil to a hot, cast-iron pot. Sauté chopped garlic, Pequins mixture, onions, jalapeño, bell pepper and half remaining lime juice. When vegetables are soft, add chicken stock, tomatoes, cilantro and remaining lime juice. Cook 15 to 20 minutes, stirring often with a wooden spoon to avoid sticking. Reduce heat to medium and add tomato sauce, TSS Southwestern Sizzler and sea salt. Continue to cook 15 to 20 minutes. Reduce heat to low to keep warm, stirring occasionally. If using cheese, add it right before serving allowing it to melt and gently blend it in.

While sauce is warming, season catfish fillets with a mild TSS all-purpose blend such as "Jalapeño Dusted™, Texas Season All, Herbal Red"™, or for a hot and spicy fillet use any of our Chili Pequin blends or Rattlesnake Dust. I used Herbal Red"™ and Rattlesnake Dust together for this recipe.

Bring an electric skillet up to 300° to 325°; add remaining 2 tablespoons olive oil and butter. Cook fillets (depending on thickness) 3 to 4 minutes on each side. Turn, using 2 spatulas to keep from breaking fillets, then season backside of fillet. Cook until meat starts to separate. If you have several fish fillets to cook, keep cooked pieces on a hot plate, uncovered, in oven on 200°.

Garnish with sliced olives and sliced avocado seasoned with TSS Rattlesnake Dust. Serve with Southwestern Sizzler Spanish Rice (page 97) and Southwestern Sizzler Beans ala Charra (page 93).

TEXAS SELECT SEASONINGS

Fish Tacos

1 pound flaky white fish (orange roughy,
    halibut, cod, mahi or tilapia)
¼ cup canola oil*
Juice of 1 lime
½ tablespoon ancho chili powder

¼ teaspoon chipotle powder
½ teaspoon Fiesta Brand® Chili Powder
¼ cup chopped fresh cilantro leaves
8 flour tortillas

Garnish:

Thinly sliced red onion
Thinly sliced scallions
Diced tomatoes

Sour cream
Hot sauce

Cabbage Salsa:

½ medium-size white cabbage, shredded
2 limes, juiced
2 mangoes, small diced
1 jalapeño, small diced

2 cups plain yogurt
2 tablespoons honey
2 tablespoons minced cilantro
Salt and Fiesta Brand® Black Pepper to taste

Combine Cabbage Salsa ingredients and set aside to blend for at least 1 hour. Preheat grill to medium-high or oven to 350°. Place fish in medium-size dish. Blend together oil, lime juice, spices and cilantro; pour over fish. Marinate 20 minutes. Remove fish from marinade and place on a hot grill or bake in oven until fish is done, about 4 to 6 minutes per side on grill or 10 to 15 minutes in the oven. Remove and let rest 5 minutes then flake with a fork. Heat tortillas in microwave 20 to 30 seconds. Divide fish among tortillas and garnish. Serve with Cabbage Salsa. Serves 4.

*For a healthier alternative, you can use Texas Pecan Oil.

RECIPE BY CHEF KEITH JONES AKA THE CHAMPAGNE CHEF
SUBMITTED BY GRAPEFEST

TEXAS

Shrimp Po'boy with Cajun Confetti Slaw

Cajun Confetti Slaw:

1 cup shredded purple cabbage
1 cup shredded green cabbage
½ cup thinly sliced red bell pepper
¼ cup chopped parsley
¼ cup sliced green onion
½ cup mayonnaise
1½ teaspoons Fiesta Brand® Cajun-All
1½ teaspoons honey
1½ teaspoons Creole mustard
½ teaspoon each Fiesta Brand® Black Pepper and salt

Shrimp Po' Boy:

1 package HEB Great Catch Spicy Fried Shrimp (frozen)
1 loaf good French bread
1 recipe Cajun Confetti Slaw
1 cup canned French fried onions

Combine slaw ingredients and mix well; set aside. Prepare shrimp per package instructions. Split bread in half lengthwise. Spread slaw evenly over bottom half of bread. Top with shrimp and onions. Cap with top of bread and press lightly so the bread can soak up some of the dressing. Serve and enjoy!!!

CHEF JUSTIN VICKERY, SHRIMPOREE, ARANSAS PASS

Southern Comfort Shrimp

1 to 2 tablespoons light oil (canola, vegetable, etc.)*
2 pounds large shrimp, peeled and deveined
1 sweet onion, sliced thin
2 small or 1 large green bell pepper, thinly sliced
3 garlic cloves, minced
Salt and Fiesta Brand® Black Pepper to taste
½ teaspoon Fiesta Brand® Cayenne Pepper
1 teaspoon dried thyme
½ cup Southern Comfort
2 cups good quality tomato sauce
2 tablespoons Creole mustard
¼ cup honey (adjust for sweetness)
3 cups cooked rice, cooked in stock (chicken or shrimp)

Heat a large, heavy skillet over medium-high heat 2 minutes. Add oil followed by shrimp. Do shrimp in two batches if pan is too crowded. Allow shrimp to just brown a little then remove to a plate and set aside. Add onion, bell pepper and garlic to pan, adding more oil if needed. Season with salt, pepper, cayenne and thyme. Increase heat to high and sauté about 5 minutes or until good caramelization has occurred. Slide veggies to perimeter of pan and deglaze with Southern Comfort (be careful of possible flame ups!!!). Scrape bottom of pan and allow liquid to reduce by ½. Add tomato sauce, mustard and honey. Simmer about 3 minutes and adjust seasoning if necessary. Put shrimp back into pot and simmer about 2 to 4 more minutes or until shrimp have finished cooking. Serve over rice and enjoy!!!

*For a healthier alternative, you can use Texas Pecan Oil.

CHEF JUSTIN VICKERY
SHRIMPOREE, ARANSAS PASS

SHRIMPOREE

June • Aransas Pass

Enjoy a variety of fun, family entertainment including live music, demonstrations by famous chefs from across the state, more than 110 Arts and Crafts vendors, and so much more. Shrimporee appeals to young and old alike with the Annual Kick-Off Parade, Outhouse Race, Coolmelt Down, Mens Sexy Legs, Shrimp Peel & Eat or Ice Sculpting Contest and many other activities. Shrimporee has been known to host over 60,000 visitors in a single weekend. Join us.

1.800.633.3028 • www.aransaspass.org

Texas Shrimp Boil

½ small bottle hot sauce
½ small bottle Worcestershire sauce
1 carrot, chopped
2 onions, chopped
2 tablespoons minced garlic
2 tablespoons liquid crab boil
1 tablespoon Fiesta Brand® Black Pepper
4 lemons, halved
4 tablespoons Fiesta Brand® Cajun-All
2 jalapeño peppers, seeded and minced
2 Fiesta Brand® Whole Bay Leaves
10 small red potatoes, whole
2 pounds smoked sausage, sliced
6 ears corn, halved
5 pounds shrimp

Combine everything, except corn and shrimp, in a large pot; add water to more than cover. Bring to a boil and cook, covered, until potatoes are beginning to tender. Add in corn. Cook until potatoes are done then add shrimp. Cook until shrimp is done. Carefully drain off water, dump the finished, drained boil onto a table covered with newspaper.

Fried Oysters

1 dozen oysters, shelled
Melted butter*
1 teaspoon Fiesta Brand® Cayenne
  Pepper

1 teaspoon salt
1 cup all-purpose flour
½ cup yellow cornmeal
Oil for frying*

Dip oysters in melted butter; sprinkle with cayenne pepper and salt. Combine flour and cornmeal. Roll seasoned oysters in flour mixture. Cook in a skillet with hot oil until golden, about 2 or 3 minutes.

*For a healthier alternative, you can use Texas Pecan Oil.

FULTON OYSTERFEST

First Weekend in March • Fulton

Sponsored by the Fulton Volunteer Fire Department and the Town of Fulton, Oysterfest is a salute to the tasty bi-valve found in our local waters. Oysterfest features carnival rides, games, food, an oyster eating contest, live music, unique vendor booths and most of all - FUN! The celebration is a labor of love for the Fulton Volunteer Fire Dept. Over the past years, they have used proceeds from the festival to purchase life-saving and fire-fighting equipment and fire trucks. Oysterfest proceeds are the major source of funding for fire protection equipment in the community. 2009 celebrates 30 years of Oysterfest.

361.729.2388 • www.fultontexas.org

Texas Crab Quiche

1 pastry shell
1 egg white
2 tablespoons minced shallots
1 cup crabmeat
1 tablespoon flour
1½ cups shredded Swiss cheese, divided
4 eggs
1 cup half and half
1 cup cooked and crumbled bacon
1 can green chiles
½ teaspoon salt
Hot pepper sauce to taste
Dash Fiesta Brand® Ground Nutmeg
Dash Fiesta Brand® Chili Powder
3 tablespoons parsley

Brush pie shell with egg white; bake about 5 minutes at 400°. Combine remaining ingredients in a bowl and pour into pie shell. Bake at 350° about 30 minutes. Allow to cool slightly before slicing.

Tex-Mex Seafood Dinner

12 corn tortillas, cut into small triangles
2 cups cooked and peeled small shrimp
1 cup crab or imitation crabmeat
1 cup small scallops
1 envelope dry onion soup mix
1½ cups salsa
1 can cream of chicken soup
1 can green chiles
½ cup chopped onions
½ cup chopped water chestnuts
1 can sliced black olives
1 teaspoon cumin powder
Dash Fiesta Brand® Cilantro
Lemon juice to taste
2 cups shredded Cheddar cheese

Treat a casserole dish with nonstick spray and layer ⅓ corn tortilla triangles in the bottom. In a saucepan, combine remaining ingredients, except cheese. Layer ½ filling over tortillas in dish then top with cheese; repeat ending with cheese. Bake at 350° about 30 minutes.

Cookies, Candies & Snacks

Mexican Wedding Cookies, page 197

Pecan Sandies

1 cup margarine, softened
1 cup vegetable oil*
1½ cups granulated sugar, divided
1 cup powdered sugar, sifted
2 eggs
½ teaspoon Fiesta Brand® Ground Nutmeg
1 teaspoon vanilla extract
4 cups all-purpose flour
1 teaspoon baking soda
1 teaspoon cream of tartar
1 teaspoon salt
2 cups chopped pecans
Whole pecans

Preheat oven to 375°. In a large bowl, cream margarine, vegetable oil, 1 cup granulated sugar and powdered sugar until smooth. Beat in eggs one at a time; stir in nutmeg and vanilla. Fold in flour, baking soda, cream of tartar and salt. Mix in chopped pecans. Roll dough into 1-inch balls and roll each ball in remaining granulated sugar. Place cookies 2-inches apart on ungreased cookie sheets. Press 1 whole pecan into top of each dough ball. Bake 10 to 12 minutes, or until the edges are golden. Remove from cookie sheets to cool on wire racks.

*For a healthier alternative, you can use Texas Pecan Oil.

Mexican Cookies

1½ tablespoons plus ½ cup
    Fiesta Brand® Cinnamon, divided
2½ cups sugar, divided
5 cups flour
3 teaspoons baking powder
½ teaspoon baking soda
Pinch salt
2 eggs, beaten
1 teaspoon vanilla
2 cups shortening

In a large mixing bowl, combine 1½ tablespoons cinnamon and 2 cups sugar with flour, baking powder, baking soda and salt; mix well. Beat in eggs, vanilla and shortening; mix with hands until well blended. Shape into grape-sized balls. Slash a cross-shaped pattern on top of each cookie and place on cookie sheet. Bake at 350° 10 to 12 minutes or until golden brown. Combine remaining ½ cup cinnamon and remaining ½ cup sugar and sprinkle over cookies while still hot. Cool slightly before removing from cookie sheet.

Mexican Wedding Cookies

1½ cups all-purpose flour
1 teaspoon baking powder
¼ teaspoon salt
3 tablespoons butter*
⅓ cup unsweetened applesauce
1½ cups powdered sugar, divided
1 large egg
2 teaspoons vanilla
¼ cup chopped pecans

In bowl, combine flour, baking powder and salt. In another bowl, combine butter and applesauce. Add ½ cup sugar, egg, vanilla and pecans; beat until smooth. Add flour mixture and beat again. Dough should be stiff but not dry. If it is too dry, add a little water. Divide dough into 2-dozen equal-sized balls. Place about 1 inch apart on cookie sheets sprayed with nonstick spray; bake at 350° for 15 minutes, or until light golden brown. Cover each cookie with powdered sugar.

*For a healthier alternative, you can use Texas Pecan Oil instead of butter.

Dang Good White Chocolate Oatmeal Cookies

1 cup butter or margarine, softened*
1 cup firmly packed brown sugar
1 cup granulated sugar
2 large eggs, beaten
2½ teaspoons vanilla extract
1 teaspoon honey

3¼ cups all-purpose flour
1 teaspoon each baking soda, baking
   powder and salt
1½ cups uncooked regular oats
2 cups white chocolate morsels
1 cup coarsely chopped pecans

Beat butter with mixer at medium speed until creamy; gradually add sugars, eggs, vanilla and honey; mix well. Slowly add in flour and remaining ingredients. Drop by spoonful onto greased baking sheets. Bake at 350° for 12 minutes.

*For a healthier alternative, you can use Texas Pecan Oil instead of butter.

Longhorn Patty Cookies

1 cup each shortening and butter*
2 cups each granulated sugar and
   brown sugar
4 eggs, beaten
4 cups all-purpose flour

2 teaspoons vanilla extract
2 cups quick oats and coconut
1 (12-ounce) package chocolate chips
2 cups each chopped pecans and
   cornflakes

Combine all ingredients in a very large bowl; mix well. Drop by ping pong-sized balls onto a greased cookie sheet. Bake at 325° about 15 minutes. Cool before serving.

*For a healthier alternative, you can use Texas Pecan Oil instead of butter.

Barbara's Honey Fruit Nut Oatmeal Cookies

½ cup margarine, melted
⅔ cup honey
1 egg, beaten
1 cup seedless raisins
½ teaspoon salt
2 cups quick-cooking oatmeal
1 teaspoon vanilla
1 cup chopped walnuts (or other nuts)
¼ teaspoon almond extract
1 cup pitted and chopped dates
½ cup chopped candied pineapple

"During the early years of my daughter Brandi's life, we didn't allow her to eat refined sugar. These cookies were a great treat when making a low-budget, 34-hour trip to Colorado to see my sister. The cookies held up well with time and seemed to improve in taste and texture. Sometimes I would use 1 cup pineapple and ½ cup coconut and eliminate the raisins."

Cream margarine; add honey and blend well. Beat in egg. Add remaining ingredients, mixing well. Drop by spoon onto greased baking sheet. Bake at 350° for 20 minutes. Makes about 3 dozen.

BARBARA RODGERS

OKSANA_NAZARCHUK/ISTOCKPHOTO/THINKSTOCK

Chocolate Nut Cornmeal Cookies

2 sticks butter*
¾ cup sugar
½ cup cocoa
1 egg, beaten
1½ cups flour

1 cup cornmeal
1 teaspoon baking powder
¼ teaspoon salt
1 tablespoon vanilla
½ cup chopped nuts

In a large bowl, cream butter, sugar and cocoa; add egg and mix well. Add remaining ingredients and mix well. Drop by teaspoons onto greased cookie sheet and bake at 350° for 12 to 15 minutes or until lightly browned.

*For a healthier alternative, you can use Texas Pecan Oil instead of butter.

Old-Fashioned Butter Sugar Cookies

2½ cups all-purpose flour
1½ teaspoons baking soda
1¼ cups butter*
2 cups sugar plus more for sprinkling on baked cookies
1 egg
1½ teaspoons vanilla
½ cup milk

Combine flour and baking soda. In a separate bowl, cream butter and 2 cups sugar. Beat in egg and vanilla; add milk. When mixed well, combine with dry ingredients. Roll dough into 1-inch round balls. Place cookies 2-inches apart onto ungreased cookie sheets and bake at 350° for 9 to 10 minutes for softer cookies (10 to 15 minutes for crunchier cookies). Remove from oven and sprinkle with sugar.

*For a healthier alternative, you can use Texas Pecan Oil instead of butter.

Texas Brownies

Brownies:

2 cups all-purpose flour
2 cups sugar
½ cup butter or margarine*
½ cup shortening
1 cup brewed coffee

¼ cup dark cocoa
½ cup buttermilk
2 eggs
1 teaspoon baking soda
1 teaspoon vanilla

Frosting:

½ cup butter or margarine*
2 tablespoons dark cocoa
¼ cup milk

3½ cups powdered sugar
1 teaspoon vanilla

Preheat oven to 400°. Treat a 17½x11-inch jelly-roll pan with nonstick spray. Combine flour and sugar. In a heavy saucepan over medium-high heat, combine butter, shortening, coffee, and cocoa; boil, stirring frequently. Pour over flour mixture. Add buttermilk, eggs, baking soda and vanilla. Mix well. Pour into prepared pan, and bake 20 minutes. While brownies are baking, prepare frosting. Combine butter, cocoa and milk in a saucepan. Heat to boiling, stirring frequently. Add powdered sugar and vanilla; mix well until frosting is smooth. Pour warm frosting over brownies as soon as you take them out of the oven. Cool.

*For a healthier alternative, you can use Texas Pecan Oil instead of butter.

German Chocolate Brownies

1 family-sized box brownie mix plus ingredients to prepare per directions

Coconut-Pecan Filling:

½ cup evaporated milk
½ teaspoon vanilla
3 tablespoons butter*
¼ cup brown sugar
¼ cup coconut flakes
¼ cup chopped pecans

Prepare brownies per directions on package and pour into a treated 9x13-inch glass baking dish. Combine milk, vanilla, butter and brown sugar in a small saucepan over medium heat stirring constantly until butter and sugar are melted. Remove from heat and stir in coconut and pecans. Pour filling over prepared brownie batter drizzling it in a zig-zag motion. Use a case (butter) knife to drag filling in a zig-zag pattern across top of brownie mixture in an interesting pattern. Bake brownies per package directions.

*For a healthier alternative, you can use Texas Pecan Oil instead of butter.

BARBARA RODGERS

Texas Pecan Squares

1 pound brown sugar
4 large eggs, beaten
1 teaspoon salt
2 cups pecan pieces

2 teaspoons vanilla
1 teaspoon honey or maple syrup
2 cups all-purpose flour
2 teaspoons baking powder

In a large saucepan, combine brown sugar and eggs. Cook over medium-low heat just until sugar is melted (do not cook eggs). Remove from heat, add remaining ingredients and mix well. Pour into a buttered, floured cookie pan that has sides. Bake 15 minutes at 350°. Check with a toothpick. Allow to cool and cut.

Lemony Raisin Oatmeal Bars

2 cups Sun-Maid raisins
1 (14-ounce) can Eagle Brand sweetened
   condensed milk
1 tablespoon lemon juice
1 tablespoon grated lemon peel
1⅓ cups packed brown sugar

¾ cup margarine or butter, softened*
1½ teaspoons vanilla extract
1 cup all-purpose flour
½ teaspoon baking soda
¼ teaspoon salt
2½ cups oats

Preheat oven to 375°. In a saucepan, combine raisins, milk, lemon juice and peel. Over medium heat, cook and stir until mixture begins to bubble; cool. Meanwhile, in mixer bowl, combine brown sugar, margarine and vanilla; beat until light and fluffy. In a separate bowl, combine flour, baking soda, salt and oats; mix well. Reserve 1½ cups and stir remaining dry mixture into brown sugar mixture. Press firmly on bottom of greased 9x13-inch baking pan. Spread raisin mixture over crust to within ½-inch of edges. Top with reserved crumb mixture; press lightly. Bake 25 to 30 minutes or until golden brown; cool and cut into bars. Store covered at room temperature.

*For a healthier alternative, you can use Texas Pecan Oil instead of butter.

JULIE ARAGON AND HER MOM, DALLAS

Lemon-Blueberry Bars

2 cups blueberries
1 tablespoon sugar
2 tablespoons fresh lemon juice
Zest of 1 lemon, divided
1 box lemon cake mix
4 eggs, divided
1 stick butter or margarine, softened*
1 (8-ounce) package cream cheese
2¾ cups powdered sugar

Combine blueberries with sugar, lemon juice and half of the lemon zest; set aside. Combine cake mix with 1 egg, softened butter and remaining lemon zest. Pat into a buttered and floured 9x13-inch baking pan. With a mixer, beat cream cheese and powdered sugar with remaining 3 eggs until smooth. Gently stir in blueberry mixture, pour over cake. Bake in a preheated 325° oven about 55 minutes, or until browned. Cool, chill then cut into squares. Store in refrigerator.

*For a healthier alternative, you can use Texas Pecan Oil instead of butter.

SHERRIE RANDALL
THE BLUEBERRY PLACE, NACOGDOCHES

TEXAS BLUEBERRY FESTIVAL
Second weekend in June • Nacogdoches

The most delicious festival in Texas celebrates its 20th anniversary in the beautiful historic downtown of Nacogdoches. The free festival features live music on three stages and more than 100 arts, crafts and food vendors. Special events include a costumed pet parade, blueberry pie eating contest, pie-making contests and bounce park. Fresh Nacogdoches County blueberries are also on sale at the festival. In 2008, 12,000 pounds of the delightful, healthy berries were sold by noon!

936.560.5533
www.texasblueberryfestival.com

BRUCE PARTAIN, NACOGDOCHES COUNTY CHAMBER OF COMMERCE

Lemon Drop Strawberry Squares

1½ sticks butter, softened*
¾ cup powdered sugar, divided
2 teaspoons vanilla
¼ teaspoon salt
2¼ cups plus ⅓ cup all-purpose flour
2 cups granulated sugar
6 eggs
2 teaspoons lemon zest
½ cup lemon juice
1 cup sliced strawberries
Chopped nuts (optional)

Combine butter, ½ cup powdered sugar, vanilla, salt and 2¼ cups flour until smooth. Press dough over bottom of 9x5-inch pan that has been oiled or sprayed with nonstick spray. Bake at 350° about 20 minutes. While crust is cooking, combine granulated sugar, ⅓ cup flour, eggs, lemon zest and juice. Mix until smooth. Spoon in berries and spread over crust. Bake at 325° about 25 minutes. When cooled, dust with remaining powdered sugar and top with chopped nuts. Cut and serve.

*For a healthier alternative, you can use Texas Pecan Oil instead of butter.

Brown Sugar Cookies

Cookies:

½ cup butter, softened*
1 tablespoon vanilla
1 cup brown sugar
2 cups flour
2 eggs, divided
½ teaspoon baking powder

Topping:

1 cup brown sugar
1 cup chopped nuts

Combine cookie ingredients, except 1 egg. Spread onto cookie sheet. Beat remaining egg and spread on top of dough. Combine topping ingredients and sprinkle over dough. Bake at 350° until light brown. Cut into squares.

*For a healthier alternative, you can use Texas Pecan Oil instead of butter.

TONY SMITH BORN IN JEFFERSON

Billie Marie's Creamy Butter Pralines

1 stick margarine
1½ cups sugar
½ teaspoon baking soda
½ cup buttermilk

Pinch salt
1 tablespoon light corn syrup
1 teaspoon vanilla
1½ cups chopped pecans

Add margarine, sugar, baking soda, buttermilk, salt and syrup to a large heavy saucepan. Cook over medium, stirring constantly, until mixture forms a firm golden ball when dropped into cold water. This takes about 10 minutes. Remove from heat; stir in vanilla and pecans. Stir until mixture losses its gloss. Drop by teaspoon onto wax paper. Cool before serving.

BILLIE MARIE WALTERS, DOUGLAS

Peanut Brittle

1 cup sugar
½ cup light corn syrup
Dash salt
1 to 1½ cups shelled, raw peanuts

1 tablespoon butter
1½ teaspoons baking soda
1 teaspoon vanilla

Grease baking sheet heavily. Combine sugar, corn syrup and salt in 3-quart casserole. Stir in peanuts. Microwave on HIGH (100%) until light brown, 8 to 10 minutes, stirring once or twice. Stir in remaining ingredients until light and foamy. Quickly spread on greased baking sheet. Spread as thin as possible for brittle candy. Cool; break into pieces. Makes about 1 pound.

TONY SMITH IN HONOR OF BELLE GOODMAN, JEFFERSON

Gooey Chocolate Nut Fudge

1¼ cups sweetened condensed milk
2 tablespoons butter*
3 cups chocolate chips
⅔ cup chopped nuts
½ cup coconut

In a saucepan, heat milk and butter until butter is melted. Stir in remaining ingredients and mix well. Line a pan with foil leaving an overhang so you can lift it out. Pour the mix in the foil-lined pan and chill until firm.

*For a healthier alternative, you can use Texas Pecan Oil instead of butter.

Cheese Fudge

2 cups butter*
1 pound processed cheese, cubed
4 (1-pound) packages powdered sugar
1 cup cocoa
1 tablespoon vanilla extract
4 tablespoons chopped peanuts

In a large saucepan, melt butter over low heat; add cheese and stir until melted. Add powdered sugar and cocoa. Stir in vanilla and nuts. Spread on cookie sheets covered in foil. Refrigerate until set. Cut and serve.

*For a healthier alternative, you can use Texas Pecan Oil instead of butter.

CHOCOLATE LOVERS FESTIVAL

October • Lexington

Spend the day surrounded by chocolate starting with a Gourmet Chocolate Pancake Breakfast and 5K Chocolate Dash. Chocolate Alley features samplings and treats for sale or view and bid on the best chocolate cakes and best chocolate desserts. A slip-n-slide, games and pony rides, rock-climbing wall, and contests will keep youngsters entertained. The Historical Log Cabin Society opens their museum and log cabins with displays of antique machines. The day ends with a very exciting chocolate-themed Fear Factor Contest. (Yes, live bugs are consumed – chocolate-covered, of course.)

979.773.4337
www.chocolateloversfestival.com

No Bake Butterscotch Peanut Butter Bites

2 cups butterscotch chips
1 cup peanut butter
2 cups cornflake cereal, not frosted

In a saucepan over low heat, melt butterscotch chips and peanut butter. Remove from heat and add cereal. Drop by the spoonful (small, bite-sized portions) onto cookie sheet lined with waxed paper; chill.

Aunt Billie's Pink Peanut Patties

2 cups sugar
½ cup Karo syrup (light corn syrup)
½ cup milk
¼ cup water
2 cups raw unsalted shelled peanuts

1 teaspoon vanilla
1 tablespoon margarine
1 cup powdered sugar
Red food coloring

In a saucepan over medium heat, cook sugar, syrup, milk and water to a soft-ball stage. Stir in peanuts, vanilla, margarine and powdered sugar. Add enough drops of red food coloring to make mixture pink. Drop by the spoonful onto wax paper, buttered foil or into mini muffin cups.

BILLIE MARIE WALTERS, DOUGLAS

Spicy Caramel Party Rice Crisp Bites

30 to 40 caramel candies
1 (12-ounce) chocolate chips
1 cup rice crisp cereal
1 tablespoon hot sauce

Unwrap caramels and place them in a large glass bowl. Melt chocolate chips in microwave. Add cereal and hot sauce. Stir until well blended. When mixed, combine with caramels and gently stir to evenly coat each caramel. Place each coated caramel on wax paper to cool.

Cinnamon Tortilla Chips

⅓ cup white sugar
⅓ cup brown sugar
1 teaspoon ground Fiesta Brand® Cinnamon
¼ teaspoon Fiesta Brand® Ground Nutmeg
Flour tortillas
Oil for frying*

Combine sugars, cinnamon and nutmeg in a large bowl. Heat oil in deep-fryer or deep skillet to 375°. Cut tortillas into strips or chip shapes like mini pizza slices. Fry 4 or 5 tortilla chips for 30 seconds on a side, until golden brown. Quickly rest on a paper towel for excess oil. While still hot, toss in sugar mix; serve warm. You can also put the mix in a bag and shake to coat.

*For a healthier alternative, you can use Texas Pecan Oil.

Baked Spicy Pecans

2 egg whites
1½ tablespoons water
½ cup sugar
¼ teaspoon salt
½ teaspoon Fiesta Brand® Cinnamon or Fiesta Brand® Ground Nutmeg
1½ pounds pecan halves

In a bowl, mix egg whites and water. In a different bowl, combine sugar, salt and cinnamon or nutmeg. Dip pecans in the egg wash and then in sugar mixture; coat evenly. Place nuts on a well-buttered cookie pan and bake 1 hour at 225°. Turn as needed.

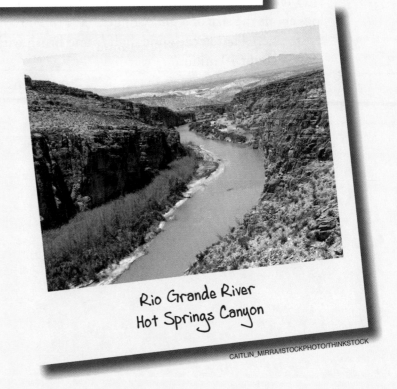

Rio Grande River
Hot Springs Canyon

Cheese Cookies

½ cup sugar
⅓ cup butter*
1 cup shredded Monterey Jack cheese
1 cup flour
2 tablespoons cornmeal
1 teaspoon baking powder
¼ teaspoon salt
1 tablespoon milk
1 large egg white

In a bowl, combine sugar and butter. Mix until creamy; add cheese. Add remaining ingredients, except egg white. Shape dough into 24 logs about the size of a pinky finger. (Or roll into one large tube and cut to size.) Flatten each one slightly and brush with egg white. Bake at 375° about 10 minutes.

*For a healthier alternative, you can use Texas Pecan Oil instead of butter.

TEXAS

Cakes, Pies & Other Desserts

Pecan Pie, page 224

Grandmother's Rocky Road Cake

Cake:

1½ squares baker's chocolate
¾ cup boiling water
½ cup margarine
1 teaspoon vanilla
¾ cup sugar
2 eggs
1 teaspoon soda
1½ cups flour
½ cup buttermilk
¾ cup brown sugar

Tony says his grandmother's recipe for Rocky Road Cake is the best cake ever. "It's my favorite cake," Tony says. This recipe is submitted by Tony and his mom in honor of his late grandmother Ruth.

Melt chocolate in boiling water and set aside. Cream margarine, vanilla and sugar together; add eggs one at a time, beating well after each. Add soda to chocolate mixture and stir. Alternately add chocolate mixture, flour and buttermilk to butter mixture, mixing well. Pour into a prepared sheet cake pan and bake at 325° for 30 to 45 minutes. Top while still hot.

Topping:

¾ cup canned milk
1½ sticks margarine
2 cups sugar
2 (6-ounce) packages chocolate chips
1 cup miniature marshmallows
1 cup chopped pecans or walnuts

Combine milk, margarine and sugar in a saucepan; bring to a boil. Remove from heat and stir in chocolate chips; continue stirring until melted. While cake is hot, coat with marshmallows and chopped nuts. Cover with chocolate sauce. Cool and serve.

TONY SMITH IN MEMORY OF RUTH GOODMAN, DIBOL

Texas Chocolate Lovers' Sheet Cake

2 cups sifted flour
1 teaspoon baking soda
½ teaspoon salt
2 cups sugar
2 sticks butter*
4 tablespoons cocoa

1 cup water
2 eggs, lightly beaten
1 teaspoon vanilla
½ cup sour cream
1 can chocolate or white icing
1 cup chopped pecans

Combine flour, baking soda, salt and sugar; set aside. Bring butter, cocoa and water to a boil in a saucepan over medium-high heat. Pour over flour mixture. Stir to mix evenly while adding eggs, vanilla and sour cream. Pour into a greased and floured deep-sided cookie sheet pan or large sheet cake pan. Bake at 350° for 20 to 25 minutes. Spread icing over cake while still hot; top with pecans.

*For a healthier alternative, you can use Texas Pecan Oil instead of butter.

Dr. Pepper Cocoa-Butter Sheet Cake

2 cups sugar

2 cups flour

½ teaspoon salt

2 sticks butter*

½ cup water

4 tablespoons cocoa

½ cup Dr. Pepper

½ cup sour cream

2 eggs

1 teaspoon baking soda

Combine sugar, flour and salt; set aside. In a small heavy pan, bring butter, water and cocoa to a boil; remove from heat. Stir in flour mixture. Add Dr. Pepper, sour cream, eggs and baking soda; mix well. Pour batter into prepared 10½x15½-inch pan. Bake at 375° for 20 to 25 minutes. Frost while cake is warm.

Frosting:

6 tablespoons milk

4 tablespoons cocoa

½ stick butter*

2 cups powdered sugar

1 tablespoon vanilla

Chopped pecans or walnuts

Boil milk, cocoa and butter until bubbly. Beat in powdered sugar and vanilla and continue to mix until smooth and creamy. Spread evenly over warm cake. Sprinkle with chopped pecans or walnuts.

*For a healthier alternative, you can use Texas Pecan Oil instead of butter.

Fresh Apple Cake "Good"

Topping:

½ stick butter*
¼ cup chopped pecans or favorite nuts
1 tablespoon brown sugar

Cake:

¼ cup shortening
1 cup sugar
2 eggs
2 cups grated apples
¼ cup water
1 cup flour
⅛ teaspoon salt
1 teaspoon baking soda
1 teaspoon Fiesta Brand® Cinnamon
½ cup chopped nuts

This recipe is so good, that according to Glynnis, her niece Besty added the word "Good" to the page the recipe was written on when she was about ten. The critique has stuck, so instead of Fresh Apple Cake this recipe is for Fresh Apple Cake "Good".

For topping, melt butter in a small saucepan; add nuts and brown sugar. Set aside. For cake, cream shortening and sugar. Add eggs, apples and water; mix well. Blend in remaining ingredients. Pour batter into a greased and floured sheet-cake pan. Sprinkle reserved topping over cake batter. Bake at 350° until cake is done.

*For a healthier alternative, you can use Texas Pecan Oil instead of butter.

SUBMITTED BY GLYNNIS SMITH, DOUGLAS

Dewberry Cake

1 cup vegetable shortening
3 eggs
2 cups sugar
1 cup dewberries (or blackberries), fresh or frozen
1 cup buttermilk
1 teaspoon baking soda
3 cups all-purpose flour
1 teaspoon salt
1 teaspoon Fiesta Brand® Ground Nutmeg
1 teaspoon Fiesta Brand® Cinnamon
1 teaspoon Fiesta Brand® Ground Cloves

Preheat oven to 350°. Grease and flour a fluted bundt pan. Cream shortening, eggs and sugar. Add berries. In a separate bowl, combine buttermilk and baking soda. In another large bowl, combine flour, salt, nutmeg, cinnamon and cloves; mix well. Add buttermilk mixture and dry ingredients alternately to creamed mixture; beat well. Pour into prepared pan. Bake 30 to 40 minutes, until a wooden pick inserted in the center comes out almost clean. Cool on a wire rack. Serves 12.

CAMERON DEWBERRY FESTIVAL

Last weekend in April • Cameron

With activities for all ages, the festival brings Wilson-Ledbetter Park to life. Activities include a barbeque cook-off, arts and crafts booths, food booths, live entertainment, horseshoe tournament, youth fishing tournament for children ages 17 and under, rides and attractions, and free dewberry cobbler and ice cream. There is also a Dewberry Cobbler and Cake Auction following the cobbler and cake contest, with monies from the auction to benefit a local charitable organization.

254.697.4979 • www.cameron-tx.com

SVETLANA TIKHONOVA/ISTOCKPHOTO/THINKSTOCK

Mom's Syrup Cake

2½ cups flour
1½ teaspoons baking soda
1 cup sugar
1 teaspoon salt
1 teaspoon Fiesta Brand® Cinnamon

1 teaspoon ginger
½ cup butter, softened (or shortening)*
1 cup syrup or molasses
2 eggs, well beaten
1 cup boiling water

Combine dry ingredients; stir in remaining ingredients. Bake at 375° in a prepared bundt pan for 25 to 30 minutes.

*For a healthier alternative, you can use Texas Pecan Oil instead of butter.

PAULETTE GOODMAN, JEFFERSON

Bluebonnets abound in Spring

DESIGN PICS/THINKSTOCK

Summer Jewel Pie

Orange Glaze:

½ cup sugar
2 tablespoons cornstarch
⅛ teaspoon salt
⅔ cup orange juice
⅓ cup water

In a saucepan, blend sugar, cornstarch and salt. Stir in orange juice and water. Cook over medium heat, stirring constantly, until mixture thickens and boils. Boil and stir 1 minute; cool.

Pie:

Short Pie Crust (see recipe next page), baked
1 cup blueberries
Orange Glaze
1½ cups sliced peaches
2 cups melon balls
½ cup sliced bananas
1 cup raspberries or sliced strawberries
Whole strawberries

Place fruits (except whole strawberries) in a bowl; pour glaze over fruits and toss lightly. Turn fruit mixture into pie crust. Garnish pie with whole strawberries. Chill before serving.

PAULETTE GOODMAN, JEFFERSON

Short Pie Crust

Paulette says, "This pie crust recipe is easy and tasty! It is a rich, cookie-like crust that is super-excellent filled with ice cream and fresh fruit."

1 cup Bisquick
¼ cup butter or margarine, softened*
3 tablespoons boiling water

Heat oven to 450°. In small mixing bowl or 9-inch pie pan combine Bisquick and butter or margarine. Add boiling water and stir vigorously until dough forms a ball and comes clean from the bowl. Dough will be puffy and soft. With fingers and heel of hand, pat dough evenly against bottom and side of pie pan. Flute edge if desired. Bake 8 to 10 minutes. Cool.

*For a healthier alternative, you can use Texas Pecan Oil instead of butter.

PAULETTE GOODMAN, JEFFERSON

Creamy Strawberry Pie

2 packages (8-ounces) cream cheese, softened
½ cup plus 2 tablespoons sugar, divided
2 eggs
¼ teaspoon almond extract
Graham cracker pie crust
½ cup sour cream
½ teaspoon vanilla
1 can strawberry pie filling

This recipe calls for strawberry pie filling but you can use any pie filling you enjoy!

Beat cream cheese, ½ cup sugar, eggs and almond extract until fluffy. Spoon into pie crust and bake at 325° for 35 to 40 minutes. Combine sour cream, 2 tablespoons sugar and vanilla; whisk until smooth. Gently spread over top of pie and bake another 5 to 8 minutes. Cool to room temperature; top with filling. Refrigerate until set. Slice and serve.

Thousand Dollar Pie

½ cup lemon juice
1 can sweetened condensed milk
1 can crushed pineapple, drained
1 cup chopped pecans
1 (4-ounce) package coconut
1 (8-ounce) carton Cool Whip
Graham cracker crust

Mix lemon juice and milk; add pineapple, nuts and coconut. Gently fold in Cool Whip. Put into a graham cracker crust. Chill 6 to 8 hours.

BELLE GOODMAN AND JUDY REAVES, DIBOL

Galveston

SERGEI KUBYSHIN/ISTOCKPHOTO

Apple & Oats Pie

Crust/Topping:

2 cups flour

1 cup brown sugar

¾ cup melted butter*

½ cup quick cooking oats

1 teaspoon cocoa

Filling:

⅔ cup sugar

3 tablespoons cornstarch

1¼ cups water

3 cups diced peeled apples

⅓ cup chopped walnuts (optional)

1 teaspoon vanilla

In a large bowl, combine crust/topping ingredients. Press ½ into a prepared 9-inch pie plate or tin. For filling, combine ⅔ cup sugar, cornstarch and water in a saucepan over medium-high heat. Stir until smooth while bringing to a slight boil. Remove from heat and stir in apples, walnuts and vanilla. Spoon into crust. Gently spread remaining crust/topping mix over top and bake at 350° for 40 to 45 minutes.

*For a healthier alternative, you can use Texas Pecan Oil instead of butter.

Deep-Dish Pecan Pie

3 eggs
1 cup corn syrup (dark or light)
½ cup sugar
¼ cup butter*

1 tablespoon vanilla
1½ cups whole and broken pecans
1 deep-dish unbaked pie shell
Vanilla ice cream

In a large bowl, beat eggs with whisk and stir in corn syrup, sugar, butter and vanilla until well mixed. Evenly spread pecans on bottom of pie shell. Pour egg mixture over pecans; smooth and bake 1 hour at 350°. Allow to cool before serving. Serve topped with vanilla ice cream.

*For a healthier alternative, you can use Texas Pecan Oil instead of butter.

Pecan Pie

4 eggs
1 cup sugar
4 tablespoons flour
1 stick butter, melted and cooled*
2 cups white corn syrup (use a 16-ounce bottle to eliminate the need to measure)
Pinch salt
4 teaspoons vanilla extract (1 tablespoon plus 1 teaspoon)
1 teaspoon almond extract
2½ to 3 cups pecans that have been cut in ½
2 pie shells, uncooked

Prior to World War II, Mary Wilson had a boarding house on Locust Street just of the square in Tyler, Texas. One of her specialties served to boarders and people that came from downtown for lunch was her pecan pie. The almond extract gives it a special flavor.

Beat eggs; add sugar and flour. Add butter, corn syrup, salt, vanilla and almond extract; mix well. Stir in pecans and fill pie shells. Bake in preheated oven at 350° about 1 hour.

*For a healthier alternative, you can use Texas Pecan Oil instead of butter.

Mary Henryitta Holloway Wilson (1888 – 1996), Omen (Smith County)

Chocolate and Pecan Lovers Pie

4 ounces semisweet chocolate, chopped
¼ stick butter*
½ cup dark brown sugar
3 large eggs, beaten

¼ teaspoon salt
¾ cup light corn syrup
1½ cups pecan pieces
1 deep-dish pie crust

Stir chocolate and butter in a saucepan over low heat until melted. In a bowl, combine brown sugar, eggs and salt; blend well. Add in corn syrup and warm chocolate mixture. Sprinkle pecans over bottom of unbaked crust. Gently pour filling over pecans. Bake at 350° until crust is golden, about 50 minutes. Cool pie completely on rack before slicing.

*For a healthier alternative, you can use Texas Pecan Oil instead of butter.

Pennybacker Bridge
(also known as Austin 360 Bridge)
Austin

RICARDO GARZA/ISTOCKPHOTO/THINKSTOCK

Yam (Sweet Potato) Pie

4 eggs
2 cups sugar
1 cup (2 sticks) butter, softened*
3 tablespoons flour
2 cups cooked mashed sweet potatoes
1½ cups milk
1 teaspoon Fiesta Brand® Cinnamon
½ teaspoon Fiesta Brand® Ground Nutmeg
½ teaspoon vanilla
1½ teaspoons orange extract
2 deep-dish (or 3 regular) pie shells

According to my mother, my great-grandmother Mary Elizabeth Martin Conley (born in Garden Valley, Texas, Smith County) made the best sweet potato pie with a hint of orange flavoring (grated orange peel). Since I do not always have an orange on hand, I use orange extract. Mother says my version is "just like Mrs. Conley's".

Mix eggs, sugar and butter until well blended. Add remaining ingredients, except pie shells, and mix well. Pour into unbaked pie shells and bake at 350° until done, about 70 minutes for regular-sized pie or 75 minutes for deep-dish pies. Test with a toothpick at 1 hour.

Note: If you usually increase the spices when baking sweet potato pie, do not for this recipe. The measurements have already been increased.

*For a healthier alternative, you can use Texas Pecan Oil instead of butter.

SANDRA FITE, GILMER

EAST TEXAS YAMBOREE

October • Gilmer

When Gilmer started hosting The East Texas Yamboree in 1935, yams (actually sweet potatoes) were a major crop in Upshur County. The Yam Pie Contest is the oldest ongoing sanctioned event sponsored by the Texas Extension Education Agency of Upshur County which also sponsors the home-canning contest. Creations of the Decorated Yam Contest are a must see exhibit. Events include two parades, barn-dance, fiddler's contest, livestock show, and more.

903.843.4019 • www.yamboree.com

Sweet Potato Pie

1 pound sweet potatoes
½ cup butter, softened*
1 cup sugar
2 eggs
½ cup milk
½ teaspoon Fiesta Brand® Ground Nutmeg
½ teaspoon Fiesta Brand® Cinnamon
1 teaspoon vanilla
1 (9-inch) pie crust, unbaked
Powdered sugar

Boil sweet potatoes whole in skin until done, about 35 to 45 minutes. Remove skin and break potatoes apart in a large bowl. Add butter, and mix well. Stir in sugar, eggs, milk, nutmeg, cinnamon and vanilla. Use an electric mixer and beat on medium speed until mixture is smooth. Spoon filling into an unbaked pie crust and bake at 350° for 1 hour. Allow pie to cool. Serve in slices topped with a few sprinkles of powdered sugar.

*For a healthier alternative, you can use Texas Pecan Oil instead of butter.

Sweet Tater Poon

1½ cups dark brown sugar, firmly packed
½ cup butter, melted*
1 large egg
½ teaspoon sugar
8 cups shredded sweet potatoes
½ cup molasses or syrup
½ cup self-rising flour

¼ cup milk
½ cup sweetened shredded coconut
½ cup dark or golden raisins
1 tablespoon vanilla extract
2 teaspoons allspice
1 teaspoon Fiesta Brand® Cinnamon
½ cup chopped pecans

Grease a 2-quart casserole dish. In a large bowl, combine brown sugar and butter. Beat in egg and add remaining ingredients, except pecans; mix well. Pour mixture into prepared dish and bake at 350° for 1½ hours or until top is browned. About 30 minutes before removing from oven top with chopped pecans.

*For a healthier alternative, you can use Texas Pecan Oil instead of butter.

Beverly's Fruit Cobbler

1 stick margarine
1 cup flour
1½ cups sugar (divided)
2 teaspoons baking powder

½ cup milk
1 quart fruit (your favorite)
1 cup water

Melt margarine and pour into a 9x13-inch dish. Combine flour, 1 cup sugar, baking powder and milk. Pour into baking dish over melted margarine. Drain fruit and combine with water and ½ cup sugar. Pour into baking dish over flour mixture. Bake at 375° for 1 hour. Best served warm with Cool Whip or vanilla ice cream.

PAULETTE GOODMAN, JEFFERSON

Tex-Mex Walnut Cranberry Crumble

2 cups cranberries
1 cup sugar (divided)
½ cup chopped walnuts
1 egg
1 teaspoon Fiesta Brand® Cinnamon
Dash hot sauce

½ teaspoon chili power
½ teaspoon cumin powder
¼ cup butter or margarine, melted*
1 cup crushed graham crackers
Vanilla ice cream

Put cranberries in a slightly greased pie plate; sprinkle with ½ cup sugar and nuts. In a bowl, beat the egg well, adding ½ cup sugar gradually until foamy. Add cinnamon, hot sauce, chili, cumin and melted butter. Beat until blended; stir in graham cracker crumbs. Spoon topping mix evenly over berries and bake 45 minutes at 325°. Crust should be a golden brown. Serve warm topped with ice cream.

Note: You can also bake this in a pie shell if desired.

*For a healthier alternative, you can use Texas Pecan Oil instead of butter.

Baked Strawberry Flan

1 cup sugar
3 eggs
1 can sweetened condensed milk
1 can evaporated milk
1 tablespoon vanilla extract
Sliced strawberries
Powdered sugar

In a saucepan over medium-low heat, melt sugar slowly until liquefied and golden in color. Do not burn. Carefully pour hot sugar syrup into a 9-inch, round glass baking dish, turning the dish to evenly coat the bottom and sides. In a large bowl, beat eggs and add in condensed milk, evaporated milk and vanilla until smooth. Pour egg mixture into sugar coated baking dish. Cover with aluminum foil. Bake at 350° for 1 hour. Cool completely. To serve, carefully cut pieces, invert to show golden color and top with a few slices of strawberries sprinkled with powdered sugar.

POTEET STRAWBERRY FESTIVAL
April • Poteet

One of the oldest, most popular events in the state, the Annual Poteet Strawberry Festival is recognized as one of the most exciting, dynamic festivals in the Greater Southwest. The 95-acre site, located on Hwy 16 just 25 miles south of San Antonio, offers free parking, clean restrooms, handicapped accessibility and complete RV facilities. Great food, arts and crafts, family entertainment, concerts featuring Country/Western and Tejano stars, a Rodeo and a world class carnival round out the weekend.

1.888.742.8144 • www.strawberryfestival.com

Cream Cheese Nanner Pudding

1 (8-ounce) package cream cheese, softened
1 can sweetened condensed milk
1 package instant vanilla pudding mix
3 cups cold milk
1 teaspoon vanilla extract
1 (8-ounce) carton whipped topping, divided
1 box vanilla wafers
4 to 5 bananas, sliced
1 cup chopped Texas-grown pecans

In a large bowl, beat cream cheese until soft. Add condensed milk, pudding mix, cold milk and vanilla extract; continue to beat until smooth. Fold in ½ of whipped topping and set aside. Line bottom of a 9x13-inch dish with vanilla wafers. Arrange sliced bananas evenly over wafers. Spread with pudding mixture. Top with remaining whipped topping; sprinkle with pecans. Chill before serving.

Fried Bananas with Cream Sauce

4 to 5 bananas
1 stick butter*
1 cup brown sugar
1 cup orange juice

Ice cream
½ cup sour cream
½ cup powdered sugar

Peel bananas; cut in half lengthwise once, then crosswise once. In a nonstick skillet, heat butter and carefully fry bananas (all at once) until golden. While bananas are frying, combine brown sugar and orange juice. Pour over bananas in skillet and simmer 10 minutes over medium heat. In serving bowls, add a scoop of ice cream and spoon bananas and sauce over ice cream. Combine sour cream, powdered sugar and a few spoonfuls of remaining liquid from skillet; mix well and top bananas. Serve quickly.

*For a healthier alternative, you can use Texas Pecan Oil instead of butter.

Quick Spicy Dulce

12 frozen yeast rolls
½ can chocolate icing
1 tablespoon hot sauce
Flour, if needed

This is a quick and easy version for a Dulce using simple ingredients and a bit of hot sauce for added kick.

Allow rolls to rise and then cook per directions on package. Combine chocolate icing with hot sauce and stir well. Add a bit of flour to thicken, if needed. Cover rolls with chocolate topping and serve.

Traditional Pan Dulce

1 tablespoon dry yeast
1 tablespoon plus ⅓ cup sugar
¼ cup warm water
3⅔ cups white bread flour

1 teaspoon salt
2 tablespoons shortening
5 large eggs, beaten

Topping:

¼ cup unsalted butter*
¼ cup shortening
1 cup powdered sugar
1 cup all-purpose flour

1 teaspoon vanilla extract
1 tablespoon lemon peel
1 tablespoon cocoa
⅛ teaspoon Fiesta Brand® Cinnamon

Dissolve yeast and 1 tablespoon sugar in warm water; set aside for 10 minutes. Add bread flour, salt, ⅓ cup sugar, shortening and eggs; mix well. You should have a workable, elastic dough. Divide dough into 2 equal portions, cover with cling wrap, and let rise in a warm place for 45 minutes. While dough is rising, begin mixing chocolate topping. Mix all topping ingredients in a food processor until smooth. Work into a log shape, chill until dough is ready. Divide pastry dough into 20 pieces and shape each into a ball. Place on a lightly greased baking sheet with plenty of space between each dough ball. Press each ball slightly to flatten it. Cut topping into 20 equal pieces. Place each piece between two sheets of wax paper and flatten until wide enough to cover pastry. Place over pastry dough. Let rolls rise again in a warm place for about an hour. Preheat oven to 350° and bake 12 to 15 minutes until browned. Serve immediately; warm leftovers before serving.

*For a healthier alternative, you can use Texas Pecan Oil instead of butter.

Chocolate Pate

1½ pounds semisweet chocolate, chopped
1¾ pounds butter, cubed*
½ pound powdered sugar
½ cup Messina Hof Papa Paulo Texas Port
9 eggs, beaten

Chocolate is an ideal pairing for port. In 1986, our wine and food experiments became our wine-based food line with jellies, mustards, port fudge sauce and port wine chocolate truffles. Each year, we add a new wine-based food product to the Messina Hof wine food line.

In the top of a double boiler, melt chocolate and butter. Whisk in powdered sugar and wine. Slowly add eggs, whisking constantly. Pour into buttered miniature loaf pans; cool. Store in refrigerator. Slice like pâté to serve. Serves 10.

*For a healthier alternative, you can use Texas Pecan Oil instead of butter.

MESSINA HOF WINE PREMIERE AS FEATURED IN
MESSINA HOF VINEYARD CUISINE COOKBOOK

Peach Ice Cream

1 quart heavy cream
1 quart half & half
2 cups sugar
¼ teaspoon salt
1 tablespoon vanilla
2 cups peeled and chopped fresh peaches

We make this when the local peach crop is at its peak. It's a favorite at church socials.

Mix cream and half & half in a large mixing bowl. Add sugar and salt; stir until dissolved. Stir in vanilla and peaches. Place in a 4-quart ice cream freezer container. Freeze until firm. Makes 1 gallon.

S. WISE, GILMER

Twice Cooked Texas Peaches in Brown Sugar and Pan Sauce

This recipe is so simple it's a bigger sin than the calories themselves! It goes great with Texas Blue Bell Ice Cream or Vanilla Gelato. Want to try something different? Garnish it with julienned basil.

Canola oil, as needed*
4 ripe Texas peaches, washed, cut in half, pitted
¼ cup brown sugar
1 tablespoon vanilla
2 teaspoons Fiesta Brand® Cinnamon
Pinch of clove
½ stick unsalted butter*

Preheat oven to 375°. Heat a sauté pan over high heat until just starting to smoke. Add a tablespoon or 2 of canola oil and then peaches, immediately, flesh-side down. LEAVE THE PEACHES ALONE! You want the natural sugars to caramelize well. After a minute turn peaches over to skin-side and cook an additional 30 seconds. Remove peaches to a cookie sheet and place in oven 10 to 15 minutes. Return sauté pan to medium-high heat; add brown sugar, vanilla, spices and butter. (Add butter last so it won't burn.) Whisk constantly being careful not to let it burn. Remove peaches from oven to plate. Pour sauce over and garnish, if desired, with toasted Texas pecan halves, ice cream and/or fresh basil. Serves 4.

*For a healthier alternative, you can use Texas Pecan Oil.

CHEF MARK McDANIEL, ReMARKable Affairs Catering
WWW.REMARKABLEAFFAIRS.COM

Baked Pears

4 ripe pears, peeled, cored, sliced
2 tablespoons brown sugar
¼ teaspoon Fiesta Brand® Cinnamon
2 tablespoons lemon juice

2 tablespoons melted butter*
¼ teaspoon maple syrup
½ cup orange juice

Place pears in a prepared baking dish. In a bowl combine brown sugar, cinnamon, lemon juice, butter and maple syrup. Spoon over pears, turning to coat. Gently pour orange juice in bottom of pan around pears and bake 25 minutes at 350°.

*For a healthier alternative, you can use Texas Pecan Oil instead of butter.

Cathy's Peach Cobbler

Crust:

2 cups all-purpose flour
1 teaspoon salt

⅔ cup shortening
5 to 6 tablespoons cold water

Mix flour and salt. Cut in shortening. Add cold water and stir with fork until mixture forms a ball. Roll out half of the mixture and line 9x9-inch baking dish.

Filling:

1 (29-ounce) can sliced peaches
3 tablespoons butter, divided*

⅔ cups plus ¼ cup sugar, divided

Place peaches on top of crust in baking dish. Dot with 2 tablespoons butter and cover with ⅔ cup sugar. Roll out remaining crust; cut into strips. Weave strips on top peaches. Dot top crust with remaining butter and sprinkle with ¼ cup sugar. Bake at 375° for 35 to 45 minutes or until golden brown.

*For a healthier alternative, you can use Texas Pecan Oil instead of butter.

ALICIA MEEVES, GRAND PRIZE WINNER,
COAL MINERS' HERITAGE FESTIVAL BAKING CONTEST, BRIDGEPORT

Texas Festivals

The following is a list of almost 400 annual festivals found throughout the Lone Star State. Chances are, we've neglected to include some events. If you aware of any we missed, call us toll-free 1.888.854.5954, and we'll do our best to include it in a subsequent printing. Keep in mind, too, that dates and venues change. Please verify all information before making plans to attend any of these events. Festivals are listed alphabetically by the city where the festival is held. Please call the number listed or visit the festival's website for more information.

Abilene • Spirit of the Frontier Festival
October • 325.437.2800 • frontiertexas.com

Abilene • City Sidewalks
December • 325.677.2281 • abilenetx.com

Addison • North Texas Jazz Festival
April • 940.565.3742 • jazz.unt.edu

Addison • Taste Addison
May • 972.450.6221 • addisontexas.net

Addison • The 500 Inc. Winefest
November • 800.233.4766 • addisontexas.net

Addison • Worldfest
October • 800.233.4766 • addisontexas.net

Albany • Chinese New Year Family Festival
February • 325.762.2269 • theoldjailartcenter.org

Anahuac • Texas Gatorfest
September • 409.267.4190 • texasgatorfest.com

Aransas Pass • Holiday on the Harbor
December • 800.633.3028 • aransaspass.org

Aransas Pass • Shrimporee
June • 800.633.3028 • aransaspass.org

Arlington • Texas Scottish Festival & Highland Games
June • 800.363.SCOT (7268)
texasscottishfestival.com

Athens • Black-Eyed Pea Fest
October • 903.675.5630 • easttexasarboretum.org

Austin • Zilker Garden Festival
March/April • 512.477.8672 • zilkergarden.org

Austin • Louisiana Swamp Thing & Crawfish Festival
April • 512.441.9015 • roadwayevents.com

Austin • Old Settlers Music Festival
April • 512.383.1748 • oldsettlersmusicfest.org

Austin • Texas Hill Country Wine and Food Festival
April • 512.249.6300 • texaswineandfood.org

Austin • Austin Chronicle Hot Sauce Festival
August • 512-454-5766
austinchronicle.com/hotsauce

Austin • Batfest
August • 512.441.9015 • roadwayevents.com

Austin • Ice Cream Festival
August • 512-923-1726 • icecreamfestival.org

Austin • First Night Austin
December • 512.391.1551 • firstnightaustin.org

Austin • Holiday Art Festival
December • 512.458.8191 • amoa.org

Austin • Chocolate Festival
September • 800.834.3498
austinchocolatefestival.com

Austin • Zilker Kite Festival
March • 512.448.KITE (5483)
zilkerkitefestival.com

Austin • Texas Craft Brewers Festival
May • txbrewersfestival.com

Austin • Texas Greek Festival
May • texasgreekfestival.com

Austin • Texas Book Festival
November • 512.477.4055
texasbookfestival.org

Austin • Austin Cave Festival
October • 512.499.2550
bseacd.org/western_oaks.htm

Austin • Texas Wine & Song Festival
October • texaswineandsong.com

Ballinger • Christmas in Olde Ballinger
November • 325.365.2333 • ballingertx.org

Bandera • Harvest Fest
November • 830.796.4447
banderacowboycapital.com

Bastrop • Harvest Art Fest
November • 512.303.9599
bastropassociationforthearts.org

Bastrop • Veterans' Day Celebration
November • 512.321.9000 • bastropdba.org

Bastrop • Bastrop State Park Fall Festival
October • 512.321.2101 • friendsoflostpines.org

Baytown • Heritage Festival
April • 281.421.2099 • baytownhistory.org

Baytown • Heritage Scaritage Festival
October • 281.421.2099 • baytownhistory.org

Beaumont • Christmas Holiday Festival
December • 800.392.4401 • beaumontcvb.com

Beaumont • Harvest Hoedown
October • 409.832.1906

Bellville • Small Town Christmas
December • 979.865.3407 • bellville.com

Bellville • Bluegrass & Gospel Music Festival
October • 979.865.5250

Belton • Market Days
November • 254.939.3551 • beltonchamber.com

Benbrook • Heritage Fest Cowboy Roundup
October • 817.249.6008 • cityofbenbrook.com

Bertram • Olde Tyme Christmas Festival
November • 512.355.2197

Blanco • Lavender Festival
June • 830.833.5101 • blancolavenderfest.com

Boerne • Berges Fest
June • 830.428.8778 • bergesfest.com

Boerne • Dickens on Main
November • 830.249.2766
boerneDickensonMain.com

Boerne • Wild West Day
October • 800.640.5917
enchantedspringsranch.com

Boerne • Harvest Moon Celebration
October • 830.249.7277 • visitboerne.org

Bowie • Fantasy of Lights Christmas Festival
December • 940.872.6246 • cityofbowietx.com

Bowie • Chicken & Bread Days Heritage Festival
October • 940.872.6246 • cityofbowietx.com

Brady • World Championship Barbecue Goat Cook-Off
August • bradytx.com

Brenham • Ice Cream Festival
May • downtownbrenham.com

Brenham • Maifest
May • maifest.org

Bridgeport • Coal Miners' Heritage Festival
October • 940.683.2076

Brownfield • Harvest Festival
October • 806.637.2564
brownfieldchamber.com

Brownsville • Charro Days Fiesta
February/March • charrodaysfiesta.com

Bryan • Texas Reds Steak & Grape Festival
June • 979.209.5528 • texasredsfestival.com

Bryan • Brazos Valley Worldfest
November • 979.862.6700
brazosvalleyworldfest.org

Buda • Budafest
December • 512.694.3413 • budafest.org

Buffalo Gap • Old Fashioned 4th of July Celebration
July • 325.572.3365

Buffalo Gap • Fall Festival
October • 325.572.3365

Burnet • Christmas Festival
December • 512.756.4297 • burnetchamber.org

Burnet • Fort Croghan Living Arts Festival
October • 512.756.8281 • burnetchamber.org

Burton • Cotton Gin Dance & Dinner Gala
October • 979.289.3378 • cottonginmuseum.org

Caldwell • Kolache Festival
September • 979.596.2383
burlesoncountytx.com

Cameron • Dewberry Festival
April • 254.697.4979 • cameron-tx.com

Canadian • Fall Foliage Festival
October • 806.323.6234

Canyon Lake • Annual Shrimp Fest
October • 830.899.4406 • clnoonlions.com

Cedar Hill • Country Day on the Hill
October • 972.291.7582
countrydayonthehill.org

Center • East Texas Poultry Festival
October • 800.854.5328
shelbycountychamber.com

Chapel Hill • Bluebonnet Festival
April • 979.836.6033
chappellhillmuseum.org/festivals.htm

Chapell Hill • Scarecrow Festival
October • 979.836.6033
chappellhillmuseum.org/festivals.htm

Clear Lake • Ballunar Liftoff Festival
October/November • 281.488.7676
ballunarfestival.com

Clear Lake • Bay Area Houston Arts Festival
October • 281.335.7777 • taaccl.org

Clifton • Fall Fest
October • 254.675.8337 • clifton.centraltx.com

Clute • Great Texas Mosquito Festival
July • 979.265.8392 • mosquitofestival.com

Clute • Harvest Fun Fest
October • 979.265.8392

Coleman • Fiesta de la Paloma
October • 325.625.2163 • colemantexas.org

Comanche • Cora's Christmas
December • 325.356.3233
comanchechamber.org

Concan • Fall Fly Fishing Fest
October • 830.591.1074 • thcrr.com

Conroe • Cajun Catfish Festival
October • 800.324.2604
conroecajuncatfishfestival.com

Conroe • Fall Festival
October • 936.756.0912 • outletsatconroe.com

Conroe • Lobsterfest
October • 936.538.7111 • conroe.org

Cooper • Delta County Chiggerfest
October • 903.395.4314 • deltacounty.org

Copperas Cove • Rabbit Fest
May • rabbitfest.com

Copperas Cove • Ogletree Gap Heritage Festival
October • 254.547.7571 • ogletreegap.net

Corpus Christi • Harbor Lights Festival
December • 361.985.1555
harborlightsfestival.com

Corpus Christi • Boar's Head & Yule Log Festival
January • 361.854.3044

Corpus Christi • Dia de los Muertos Festival
November • 361.947.6895
kspacecontemporary.org

Corpus Christi • Hispanic Heritage Festival
October • 361.289.0111 • ksabfm.com

Corpus Christi • Texas Jazz Festival
October • 254.675.8337

Crockett • World Championship Fiddlers' Festival & Steak Cook-Off
June • 888.269.2359 or 936.544.2359

Crystal Beach • Texas Crab Festival
May • 409.684.5940 • crystalbeach.com

Cuero • Turkeyfest Celebration
October • 361.275.2112 • cuero.org

Dallas • Taste of Dallas
July • 214.991.0199 • tasteofdallas.org

Dallas • North Texas Irish Festival
March • 214.821.4173 • ntif.org

Dallas • Savor Dallas
March • 866.277.7920 • SavorDallas.com

Dallas • Beaujolais Wine Festival
November • 972.241.0111 • faccdallas.com

Dallas • Chile Pepperama
November • 972.943.4624 • chilepepperama.net

Dayton • Dayton Ole Tyme Festival
April • oletymefestival.com

Dayton • Country Christmas
December • 936.336.5736
libertydaytonchamber.com

De Leon • Peach & Melon Festival
August • deleonpeachandmelonfestival.com

Denison • Main Street Fall Festival
October • 903.464.4452 • cityofdenison.com

Denton • North Texas Book Festival
April • 940.565.0804 • ntbf.org

Denton • Holiday Lighting Festival
December • 940.349.8529 • dentonlive.com

Devine • Fall Festival
October/November • 830.663.2739
devinecoc.org

Dickinson • Festival of Lights
November • 281.337.2489
dickinsonfestivaloflights.org

Driftwood • Rhythm & BBQ Festival
October • 512.444.9885 • rhythmandbbq.com

Dripping Springs • Chili Cook-Off
October • 512.858.7725

Dublin • Dr Pepper Birthday Celebration
June • 888.398.1024 • dublindrpepper.com

Eagle Pass • Christmas/Festival de Luces
November • 830.773.4343

East Bernard • Czech Kolache Klobase Festival
June • 979.335.7907 • kkfest.com

Edna • Texana Chili Spill -
November • 361.782.5456
brackenridgepark.com

Edom • Festival of the Arts
October • 903.852.3990
edomfestivalofthearts.com

El Paso • Pro Musica Chamber Music Festival
January/February • 915.833.9400
elpasopromusica.org

El Paso • Fan Fiesta
December • 915.534.0600

Elgin • Holiday by the Tracks
December • 512.281.5724 • elgintx.com

Elgin • Hogeye Festival
October • 512.281.5724 • elgintx.com

Elm Mott • Homestead Craft & Children's Fair
November • 254.754.9600
homesteadheritage.com

Ennis • Czech Music Festival
February • 972.878.4748 • visitennis.org

Ennis • National Polka Festival
May • nationalpolkafestival.com

Ennis • Autumn Days in Ennis Fall Festival
October • 972.878.4748
visitennis.org

Farmersville • Old-Time Saturday Festival
October • 972.782.6533
farmersvillechamber.com

Flatonia • Czhilispiel XXXVI
October • 361.865.3920
czhilispielfestival.com

Flatonia • Sacred Heart Fall Festival
October • 361.865.3920
flatoniachamber.com

Floresville • Peanut Festival
October • floresvillepeanutfestival.org

Fort Davis • Frontier Christmas Celebration
December • 432.426.3015 • fortdavis.com

Fort Worth • Dia de los Muertos Festival
November • 817.624.8333
rosemarinetheater.com

Fort Worth • Fall Festival in the Japanese Garden
October • 817.871.7686 • fwbg.org

Fort Worth • Gran Festival de Autos
October • granfestivaldeautos.com

Fort Stockton • Old Timers Day & Guacamole Contest
October • 432.336.2167

Fort Worth • Red Steagall Cowboy Gathering & Western Swing Festival
October • 888.269.8696 • redsteagall.com

Fredericksburg • Weihnachten
December • 888.997.3600 • tex-fest.com

Fredericksburg • Food & Wine Fest
October • 866.839.3378
fbgfoodandwinefest.com

Fredericksburg • Lone Star Gourd Festival
October • texasgourdsociety.org

Fredericksburg • Oktoberfest
October • 830.997.4810 • oktoberfestinfbg.com

Friona • Cheeseburger Cookoff Festival
July • 806.250.3491 • frionachamber.com

Frisco • Lone Star Storytelling Festival
October • friscostorytellingfestival.org

Fulton • Oysterfest
March • 361.729.2388 • fultontexas.org

Galveston • Dickens on The Strand
December • 409.765.7834
dickensonthestrand.org

Galveston • Harbor Parade of Lights & Boat Festival
December • 409.763.7080

Galveston • Mardi Gras! Galveston
February • 888.425.4753
mardigrasgalveston.com

Galveston • Festival of Lights
November • 800.582.4673 • moodygardens.com

Galveston • Seaside Treasure Festival
November • 409.744.4526 • moody.org/stf

Galveston • ARToberFEST
October • 409.762.3617 • artoberfest.com

Galveston • Greek Festival
October • 409.762.7591

George West • Storyfest
November • 361.449.2481
georgeweststoryfest.org

Georgetown • Up the Chisholm Trail Event and Chuck wagon Cook-off
September • wchm-tx.org

Georgetown • A Taste of Georgetown
October • 512.868.8675 • dgagtx.com

Gilmer • Yulefest
December • 903.843.2413
gilmerareachamber.com

Gilmer • East Texas Yamboree
October • 903.843.4019 • yamboree.com

Gladewater • Christmas Tyme in "Gusherville"
November/December • 903.845.5501
gladewaterchamber.com

Gladewater • Gusher Days
April • 903.845.5501 • gusherdays.com

Glen Rose • Pumpkin Festival
October • 888.346.6282 • glenrosetexas.net

Golden • Sweet Potato Festival
October • 903.765.2444
goldensweetpotatofestival.org

Gonzales • Come & Take It Festival
October • 888.672.1095 • gonzalestexas.com

Granbury • Country Christmas Celebration
November • 817.573.5299 • hgma.com

Granbury • Harvest Moon Festival
October • 817.573.5299 • hgma.com

Grand Prairie • Prairie Dog Chili Cook-Off and World Championship of Pickled Quail Egg Eating
April • 972.647.2331 • tradersvillage.com

Grand Prairie • Cajun Festival
May • 972.647.2331 • tradersvillage.com

Grand Prairie • Mountain Man Weekend
November • 972.647.2331 • tradersvillage.com

Grand Prairie • International Bar-B-Que Cookers Association Cook-Off
October • 972.647.2331 • tradersvillage.com

Grapevine • Nash Farm Fall Roundup
October • 817.410.3185 • grapevinetexasusa.com

Grapevine • Grapefest
September • 817.410.3195
GrapevineTexasUSA.com

Gruene • Texas Clay Festival
October • 830.629.7975 • texasclayfestival.com

Gruene • Texas Metal Arts Festival
September • 903.852.3311 • texasmetalarts.com

Hallettsville • Festival of Lights
November • 361.798.2662 • hallettsville.com

Hallettsville • Falling Leaves Polka Festival
October • 361.798.4333 • kchall.com

Harlingen • Riofest
April • 800.746.3378

Harlingen • Rio Grande Valley Birding Festival
November • 800.531.7346 • rgvbirdfest.com

Hempstead • Hardin County MusicFest
September/October • wallercountyfair.org

Henderson • Heritage Syrup Festival
November • 903.657.4303 • depotmuseum.com

Hico • Texas Steak Cookoff, Beef Symposium & Tourist Trap
May • 254.485.2020 • texassteakcookoff.com

Hillsboro • Middlefaire Renaissance Festival
October • 254.548.6238 • middlefest.com

Holland • Corn Festival
June • 254.760.3204 • hollandcornfest.org

Hondo • Christmas in God's Country
November • 830/426.3037 • hondochamber.com

Houston • Houston es Musica Festival
October/November • 713.437.5233
houstonesmusica.com

Houston • International Quilt Festival
October/November • quilts.com

Houston • Spring into Summer Doll Festival
April • 281.614.0077 • bayareadollclub.com

Houston • The Houston International Jazz Festival
August • jazzeducation.org

Houston • ClayHouston Festival
December • 713.263.1919 • clayhouston.org

Houston • Country Roots Music Festival
May • 281.890.5500 • tradersvillage.com

Houston • Highland Games and Celtic Festival
May • 713.871.0061
houstonhighlandgames.com

Houston • The Original Greek Festival
November • 713.526.5377 • greekfestival.org

Houston • Via Colori Street Painting Festival
November • 713.523.3633
HoustonViaColori.com

Houston • Asian-American Festival
October • asianfestivalhouston.com

Houston • Day of the Dead
October • 281.890.5500 • tradersvillage.com

Houston • Festa Italiana
October • houstonitalianfestival.com

Houston • Texas Renaissance Festival
October • 800.458.3435 • texasrenfest.com

Houston • Women's Festival
October • 713.995.5251 • hwfestival.org

Hughes Springs • Fall Festival
October • 903.639.1318

Huntsville • General Sam Houston Folk Festival
May • 936.294.1832

Hutto • Old Tyme Days
October • 512.759.4400 • hutto.org

Idalou • Apple Butter Festival
September • 806.781.1753
applecountryorchards.com

Ingleside • Enchanted Forest Renaissance Faire
December • 361.776.2906 • renfaireingleside.org

Ingleside • Round Up Days
October • 361.776.2906 • roundupdays.org

Irving • Le Festival de Musique!
January • 972.252.4800 • lascolinassymphony

Irving • Heritage Festival
June • irvingheritagefestival.com

Jacksboro • Bluegrass Festival
October • jacksborochamber.com

Jacksonville • Tomato Festival
June • 800.376.2217 • jacksonvilletexas.com

Jasper • Azalea Festival
March • 409.384.2762 • jaspercoc.org

Jasper • Fall Festival
October • 409.384.2762 • jaspercoc.org

Jefferson • Mardi Gras Upriver
February • 903.665.2672 • jefferson-texas.com

Jefferson • Bayou BBQ Cook-Off
July • 888.467.3529 • jefferson-texas.com

Jefferson • Pilgrimage Tour of Homes & Spring Festival
May • 903.665.2513

Jefferson • Taste of Jefferson
October • 903.665.2672 • jefferson-texas.com

Jewett • Fall Frolic
October • 903.626.4202 • jewetttexas.com

Johnson City • Pig Roast
October • jcpigroast.org

Jonestown • Oktoberfest
October • 512.267.3243 • jonestown.org

Katy • Life is Good Pumpkin Festival
October • 281.395.2200
newlandpumpkinfestival

Kaufman • Scarecrow Festival
October • 972.932.3118 • kaufmanchamber.com

Kerens • Cotton Harvest Festival
October • 903.396.2391

Kerrville • Folk Festival
May/June • 830.257.3600
kerrvillefolkfestival.com

Kerrville • Wine and Music Festival
August/September • kerrville-music.com

Kerrville • Easter Fest
March • kerrvilletexascvb.com

Kerrville • Texas Arts & Crafts Fair
May • 830.896.5711 • tacef.com

Kilgore • Party in the Patch
April • 903.984.5571 • easttexastreatment.org

Kingsville • South Texas Wildlife & Birding Festival
November • 361.592.8516 • kingsvilletexas.com

Kyle • Fair & Music Festival
October • kylefair.com

La Porte • Sylvan Beach Fest & Crawfish Jam
April • 281.471.1123 • laportechamber.org

La Porte • Fall Back Festival
October • 832.771.7661 • fallbackfestival.com

Lake Dallas • Mardi Gras Celebration
February • 940.497.2226 • lakedallas.com

Lampassas • Spring Ho Festival
July • 512.556.5301 • SpringHo.com

Lancaster • OktoberFest
October • LancasterOktoberFest.com

Laredo • Washington's Birthday Celebration
January/February • 956.722.0589
wbcalaredo.org

Laredo • International Sister Cities Festival
January • 800.361.3360

League City • Holiday in the Park Parade & Festival: Christmas on the Creek
December • 281.332.3961 • holidayinthepark.org

League City • South Shore Dockside Food & Wine Festival
October • 281.338.7339 • southshorefestival.com

Lewisville • Holiday at the Hall Festival
December • 972.219.3401 • cityoflewisville.com

Lexington • Chocolate Lovers Festival
October • 979.773.4337
chocolateloversfestival.com

Liberty • Country Christmas
December • 936.336.5736
libertydaytonchamber

Liberty • Jubilee
March • 936.336.3684
libertydaytonchamber.com

Liberty • Fall Fest
October • 936.336.6401

Linden • Wildflower Trails of Texas Festival
April • 903.756.7774 • lindenwildflowertrails.com

Linden • Winterfest
December • 903.756.3106

Linden • T-Bone Walker Blues Festival
June • tbonewalkerbluesfest.com

Livingston • Hometown Christmas
December • 936.327.1050

Llano • Heritage Days & Chuck-Wagon Cook-Off
October • 325.247.4265
llanochuckwagoncookoff.com

Llano • Heritage Festival
October • 325.247.5354 • llanochamber.com

Lockhart • Chisholm Trail Roundup BBQ & Music Festival
June • 512.398.2818 • chilsholmtrailroundup.com

Longview • AlleyFest
June • 903.237.4000 • alleyfest.org

Longview • Harvest Festival
October • 903.236.8428

Longview • Multicultural Festival
October • 903.237.1019

Lubbock • Pancake Festival
February • 800.692.4035 • lubbocklions.org

Lubbock • National Cowboy Symposium & Championship Chuckwagon Cook-Off
September • cowboy.org

Luckenbach • Blues Festival
January • 830.997.3324 • luckenbachtexas.com

Lufkin · Gallery in the Pines Fine Art Festival
November · 936.634.6305 · visitlufkin.com

Lufkin · Southern Hushpuppy Championships
September · 936.634.6305 · visitlufkin.com

Lufkin · Texas State Forest Festival
September · 936.634.6644 · texasforestfestival.com

Luling · Watermelon Thump
June · 830.875.3214 · watermelonthump.com

Luling · Zedler Mill Catfish Cook-Off & Rubber Duck Race
October · 830.875.3214 x4 · zedlermill.com

Madisonville · Texas Mushroom Festival
October · 936.348.3592
texasmushroomfestival.com

Manor · Lions Fest
October · 512.272.4247

Mansfield · Hometown Holidays & Historic Downtown Parade
December · 817.804.5785 · mansfield-tx.gov

Marshall · Fireant Festival
October · 903.935.7868 · marshalltxchamber.com

Mason · Old Yeller Days Festival
October · 325.347.5758 · masontxcoc.com

McDade · Heritage Day
October · 512.281.4651

McKinney · Dickens of a Christmas
November · 972.547.2660
downtownmckinney.com

McKinney · Festival of Trees
November · 214.544.4630 · projgrad.com

McKinney · Family Fall Festival
October · 972.547.7480 · mckinneytexas.org

Mercedes · Rio Grande Valley Music Festival
February · 956.373.0130 · rgvmf.com

Mercedes · Smokin' on the Rio
February · smokinontherio.com

Mesquite · Real Texas Festival
April · realtexasfestival.com

Midland · Septemberfest
September · museumsw.org

Midlothian · Fall Festival
October · 972.723.8600 · midlothianchamber.org

Mineola · Iron Horse Fall Fest
November · 903.569.2087 · mineolachamber.org

Mineral Wells · Crazy Water Festival
October · 940.325.0966 · crazywaterfestival.com

Mission · Citrus Fiesta
January · 956.585.9724 · Texascitrusfiesta.net

Mission · Texas Butterfly Festival
October · 956.585.2727 · missionchamber.com

Missouri City · Snowfest
December · 281.403.8500 · missouricitytx.gov

Mount Vernon · Downtown Christmas Festival
December · 903.537.4365

Mt. Pleasant · Midnight Jubilee
May · 903.572.8567 · mtpleasanttx.com

Muenster · GermanFest
April · 800.942.8037 · germanfest.net

Nacogdoches · Texas Blueberry Festival
June · 936.560.5533 · texasblueberryfestival.com

Nacogdoches · Nine Flags Festival
November · 888.653.3788 · nineflagsfestival.com

Nederland · Heritage Festival
March · 409.722.0279

Needville · Harvest Festival
October · 979.793.4030

New Braunfels · Wurstfest
October/November · 800.221.4369
wurstfest.com

Odessa · CeltFesTexas
October · 432.758.3484

Old Town Spring · Texas Crawfish & Music Festival
April · 800.Old Town · texascrawfishfestival.com

Orange · Mardi Gras Festival
February · 409.883.3536

Orange · Heritage House Past Times Days
October · 409.886.5385
heritagehouseoforange.org

Palacios · Texas Fishermen's Seafood Festival
October/November · 361.972.2615
texasfishermensfestival.com

Palestine · Fall Oktoberfest
October · 903.729.6066 · palestinechamber.org

Parker County · Peach Festival
July · 888.594.3801 · weatherford-chamber.com

Pasadena · Strawberry Festival
May · 281.991.9500 · strawberryfest.org

Pearland · Hometown Christmas Festival
December · pearlandparks.com

Pearland · Winterfest
Mid-January · 281.652.1673 · pearlandparks.com

Pearsall · Los Cazadores North American Carne Guisada Cook=Off Championship
July · 830.334.5959 · loscazadores.com

Pearsall · Potato Fest
May · 830.334.9414 · pearsalltexas.com

Pflugerville · Pfall Chili Pfest
November · 512.990.4363
cityofpflugerville.com/chili

Pilot Point · Sharkarosa Wildlife Ranch Fall Festival
October · 940.686.4600 · sharkarosa.com

Plano · Balloon Festival
September · 972. 867.7566 · planoballoonfest.org

Plantersville · Texas Renaissance Festival
October/November · 800.458.3435
texrenfest.com

Port Aransas · Texas Sand Sculpture Festival – SandFest
April · texassandfest.com

Port Arthur · Las Posada
December · 409.548.0178 · portarthurtexas.com

Port Arthur · Mardi Gras Weekend
February · 409.721.8717
portarthur.com/mardigras

Port Aransas · Fallback Festival
November · 361.749.6405

Port Lavaca · Festival by the Bay
November · 361.552.6070

Portland • WindFest
April • 361.673.2475 • windfest.org

Poteet • Strawberry Festival
April • 888.742.8144 • strawberryfestival.com

Richardson • Cottonwood Art Festival
May • cottonwoodartfestival.com

Richardson • Wildflower Arts and Music Festival
May • 972.744.4580 • wildflowerfestival.com

Rockport • Christmas by the Bay Christmas Festival
December • 361.729.6445

Rockport • Gospel Music Festival
January • 361.790.1105

Rockport • Festival of Wine & Food
May • 866.729.2469 • texasfestivalofwines.com

Rockport • Seafair
October • 361.729.6445 • rockportseafair.com

Rockport • Hummer/Bird Festival
September • 800.242.0071
rockporthummingbird.com

Round Top • Wine Tasting Festival
October/November • 979.249.4042
roundtop.org

Round Rock • Daffodil Festival
March • rrdaffodilcapitaltx.us

Royse City • Christmas Parade & Chili Cook-Off
December • 972.636.5000
roysecitychamber.com

Royse City • FunFest
October • 972.636.5000 • roysecitychamber.com

Sachse • Fallfest
October • 972.496.1212 • sachsechamber.com

Salado • Gathering of the Clans
November • 254.947.5232 • ctam-salado.org

San Angelo • Fete Festival
January/February • 325.949.4400

San Antonio • Mariachi Vargas Extravaganza
November/December • mariachimusic.com

San Angelo • Concho Valley Bluegrass Festival
April • 325.655.3821 • conchokids.org

San Antonio • Fiesta San Antonio
April • 877.723.4378 • fiesta-sa.org

San Saba • Christmas on the Square
December • 325.372.5144

San Augustine • El Camino Christmas Festival
December • 936.275.3610 • sanaugustinetx.com

San Antonio • Asian Festival
January • 210.458.2329 • texancultures.com

San Antonio • Texas Folklife Festival
June • 210.458.2224 • texancultures.com

San Antonion • Birding, Nature Festival
May • wildfestsanantonio.com

San Antonio • Cajun French Music & Food Fest
May • defatrascajun.com

San Angelo • Festival on the Concho
May • 325.374.8227 • sajuniorleague.com

San Antonio • Tejano Conjunto Festival
May • guadalupeartsfestival.org

San Antonio • New World Wine & Food Festival
November • 210.822.9555 • nwwff.org

San Felipe • Novemberfest
November • 979.885.4121

San Marcos • Veterans Day Celebration
November • 888/200.5620 • toursanmarcos.com

San Marcos • World United Music Festival
November • 512.392.4997
worldunitedmusicfestival.com

San Juan • City of Palms
October • 956.984.9468 • txmusicfestivals.com

San Augustine • Sassafras Festival
October • 936.275.3610 • sanaugustinetx.com

Schulenburg • Schulenburg Festival
August • schulenburgfestival.org

Seguin • Pecan Fest & Heritage Days
October • 800.580.7322

Seymour • Fish Day
May • 940.889.2921 • seymourtxchamber.org

Shelby County • What-a-Melon Fest
June • 936.269.9088 • shelbycountychamber.com

Sherman • Snowflake Parade & Festival
December • 903.957.0310 • shermantx.org

Sinton • San Patricio 4-H Fall Festival & Chili Cook-Off
October • 361.364.6234

Smithville • Festival of Lights
December • 512.237.2313 • smithvilletx.org

Somerville • Somerfest
October • 979.272.1835

South Padre Island • International Music Festival
October/November • 956.668.7740
spimusicfest.com

South Padre Island • Kite Festival
November • 956.761.7028

Southlake • Oktoberfest
October • 817.481.8200 • southlakechamber.com

Spring • Springfest
March • 800.653.8696 • oldtownspring.com

Stephenville • DairyFest
June • 254.965.2406 • tricountyag.com

Stonewall • Peach JAMboree and Rodeo
June • 830.644.2735 • stonewalltexas.com

Sulphur Springs • Christmas in Heritage Park
November • 888.300.6623 or 903.885.2387
sulphursprings-tx.com

Sweet Home • Chicken and Polka Fest
July • 361.798.5759 • sweethomehall.com

Taylor • International Barbeque Cook-off
August • 512.352.6364 • taylorjaycees.org

Teague • Parkfest
October • 254.739.2061

Temple • Bloomin Temple Festival
April • 254.298.5610 • bloomintemple.com

Temple • Czech Feszt
October • 254.298.5610

Terlingua • International Chili Championship
October • 210.887.8827 • chili.org

Terrell • Heritage Jubilee
April • 972.563.5703 • terrelltexas.com

Texarkana • Twice as Bright Festival of Lights
December • 870.774.2120
mainstreettexarkana.org

Texas City • FunFest
June • 409. 935.1408 • texascitychamber.com

Texas City • Model Train Festival
November • 409.643.5799 • texas-city-tx.org

The Woodlands • Red, Hot and Blue Festival and Fireworks Extravaganza
July • redhotblue.org

The Woodlands • Children's Festival
November • 281.210.1113 • woodlandscenter.org

The Woodlands • International Winter on the Waterway
November • 877.963.2447
iwowinthewoodlands.com

Three Rivers • Salsa Festival
April • 888.600.3115 • threeriverssalsa.com

Tomball • German Christmas Market
December • 281.379.6844 • tomballsistercity.org

Tomball • German Heritage Festival
March • 281.379.6844 • tomballsistercity.org

Tyler • Texas Rose Festival
October • 903.597.3130 • texasrosefestival.com

Tyler • Tiger Fest
October • 903.858.1008 • tigercreek.org

Vanderpool • St. Mary's Catholic Church Fall Festival
November • 830.966.6102

Victoria • Black History Festival
February • 361.578.6325

Vidor • Texas Bar-B-Q Festival
April • 409.769.6339 • vidorchamber.com

Waco • Fall Festival Week
October/November • 254.752.4371
artcenterwaco.org

Washington • Texas Independence Day Celebration
February/March • 936.878.2214
birthplaceoftexas.com

Waxahachie • Scarborough Renaissance Festival
April/May • 972.938.3247
scarboroughrenfest.com

Waxahachie • Downtown Victorian Christmas Festival
November/December • 972.937.2390
waxahachiechamber.com

Waxahachie • "Texas Country Reporter" Festival
October • 972.937.2390
waxahachiechamber.com

Weatherford • Veterans Day Parade
November • 817.594.4101 • visitweatherford.com

Weslaco • Texas Rio Grande Valley Onion Festival
April • 956.968.2102 • weslaco.com

Weslaco • Winter Fest
December • 956.973.3172

Weslaco • Family Fall Nature Days
November • 956/969.2475
valleynaturecenter.org

Wharton • Freedom Festival
June • 979.532.1862

Whitehouse • Four Winds Faire Renaissance Festival
February/April • 903.839.5271
fourwindsfaire.com

Whitesboro • Peanut Festival
October • 903.564.3331
whitesborotx.com

Whitewright • Fall Festival on Grand Street
November • 903.364.2000 • whitewright.org

Wichita Falls • Arts Alive! Home & Garden Festival
February • 940.767.2787 • kempcenter.org

Wichita Falls • Shrimp & Wine Festival
October • 940.322.4525 • downtownproud.com

Wills Point • Bluebird Festival
April • 800.972.5832 • willspoint.org

Winnie • Texas Rice Festival
October • 409.296.4404 • texasricefestival.org

Woodville • Festival of the Arts
March • 409.283.2272 • heritage-village.org

Woodville • Tyler County Dogwood Festival
March • tylercountydogwoodfestival.org

Yoakum • Land of Leather Days
February • 361.293.2309

Yoakum • Tom-Tom Festival
June • 361.293.2309 • victoriachamber.org

Yorktown • Western Days Festival
October • 361.564.2661 • yorktowntx.com

Index

TEXAS

YENWEN LU/ISTOCKPHOTO/THINKSTOCK

Hometown Cookbook

CLIP AND SAVE!

YOU'RE GOING TO NEED SOME AUTHENIC TEXAS SEASONINGS FOR THAT AUTHENTIC TEXAS COOKIN'! TRY SOME OF OUR DELICIOUS SPICE BLENDS TO ADD THAT LITTLE SOMETHING EXTRA TO YOUR FAVORITE DOWN-HOME DISHES!

More Great American Cookbooks

Eat & Explore Cookbook Series

Discover community celebrations and unique destinations, as they share their favorite recipes.

Explore the distinct flavor of each state by savoring 200 favorite local recipes. In addition, fun festivals, exciting events, unique attractions, and fascinating tourist destinations are profiled throughout the book with everything you need to plan your family's next getaway.

EACH: $18.95 • 256 pages • 8x9 • paperbound

Arkansas • Minnesota • North Carolina Ohio • Oklahoma • Virginia • Washington

State Back Road Restaurants Series

Every Road Leads to Delicious Food.

From two-lane highways and interstates, to dirt roads and quaint downtowns, every road leads to delicious food when traveling across our United States. Each well-researched and charming guide leads you to the state's best back road restaurants. No time to travel? No problem. Each restaurant shares their favorite recipes—sometimes their signature dish, sometimes a family favorite, always delicious.

EACH: $18.95 • 256 pages • 7x9 • paperbound • full-color

Alabama • Kentucky • Tennessee • Texas

It's So Easy...

Kitchen Memories Cookbook

Your Recipe for Family Fun in the Kitchen

This kids' cookbook and free-style memory book guarantees hours of fun and a lifetime of memories for your family. It's a cookbook, a memory book, and an activity book—all in one! A cherished keepsake for your family.

Family Favorite Recipes

It's so easy to cook great food your family will love with 350 simply delicious recipes for easy-to-afford, easy-to-prepare dinners. It's so easy to encourage your family to eat more meals at home...to enjoy time spent in the kitchen... to save money making delicious affordable meals...to cook the foods your family loves without the fuss...with *Family Favorite Recipes*.

EACH: $18.95 • 248 to 256 pages • 7x10 • paperbound • full-color

www.GreatAmericanPublishers.com • www.facebook.com/GreatAmericanPublishers

TEXAS